# Hard Times

## FOR THESE TIMES

*Based on the novel by Charles Dickens*

## HEIDI STILLMAN

NORTHWESTERN UNIVERSITY PRESS
EVANSTON, ILLINOIS

Northwestern University Press
Evanston, Illinois 60208-4210

Printed in the United States of America
10 9 8 7 6 5 4 3 2 1

ISBN 0-8101-2038-0

LIBRARY OF CONGRESS
CATALOGING-IN-PUBLICATION DATA

Stillman, Heidi.
  Hard times for these times : based on the
novel by Charles Dickens / Heidi Stillman.
    p. cm.
  ISBN 0-8101-2038-0 (pbk. : alk. paper)
  1. Social problems—Drama. 2. England—
Drama. I. Dickens, Charles, 1812–1870.
Hard times. II. Title.
  PS3619.T55 H37 2003
  813'.6—dc21

                          2002153936

Front cover: Sissy (Lauren Hirte), Lookingglass Theatre, copyright © Michael Brosilow

Back cover: Coketown, Lookingglass Theatre, copyright © Michael Brosilow

# CONTENTS

# PHOTOGRAPHS

# PRODUCTION HISTORY

The world premiere of *Hard Times: For These Times,* adapted and directed by Heidi Stillman, was produced by Lookingglass Theatre Company, Chicago, and opened on May 5, 2001.

## PRODUCTION STAFF

Set Design......................................Daniel Ostling
Lighting Design.........................Brian Sidney Bembridge
Costume Design..............................Mara Blumenfeld
Sound Design/Composition......Andre Pluess and Ben Sussman
Ariel Choreographer..................Sylvia Hernandez-DiStasi
Production Manager..........................Thomas C. Fowlkes
Production Stage Manager.......................Sara Gmitter
Prop Master.....................................Tracy Otwell
Assistant Director................................Tracy Walsh

## CAST

Mrs. Sparsit, Stephen's Wife, Pufflerumpus.............Eva Barr
Stephen, Sleary....................................David Catlin
Rachael, Mrs. Gradgrind, Scherezade................Laura Eason
Mr. Gradgrind, Sissy's Father, Slackbridge........Raymond Fox
Bitzer, Amore....................................Tony Hernandez
Sissy...............................................Lauren Hirte
Louisa...........................................Louise Lamson
Tom.................................................Joe Sikora
Mr. Harthouse, Mrs. Pegler,
Mr. M'Choakumchild, Kidderminster...........Philip R. Smith
Mr. Bounderby......................................Troy West

The second Lookingglass production opened on September 29, 2002, with the same production staff but with Rachel Carson as prop master.

CAST

Rachael, Mrs. Gradgrind, Scherezade .................... Eva Barr

Stephen, Sleary ......................................... David Catlin

Mr. Gradgrind, Sissy's Father, Slackbridge ........ Raymond Fox

Bitzer, Amore ..................................... Tony Hernandez

Sissy ............................................... Lauren Hirte

Louisa ............................................. Louise Lamson

Mrs. Pegler ......................................... Joyce Piven

Mrs. Sparsit, Stephen's Wife,
Pufflerumpus ............................... Barbara Robertson

Tom ................................................ Joe Sikora

Mr. Harthouse, Mr. M'Choakumchild,
Kidderminster ............................... Philip R. Smith

Mr. Bounderby ....................................... Troy West

# DESIGN AND STAGING

The Lookingglass Theatre set included two two-story, open-frame-work steel colonnades pivoting on castors. The bottom story of the colonnades consisted of two archways on each side, through which actors could enter or in which scenes could be played. The second floor was a playing area, open toward the front with old factory-style windows on the upstage side. The colonnade unit was the full width of the stage and near the height of the stage. The units pivoted from the downstage/offstage corners of the stage (although there was a narrow playing space downstage of the colonnades in the closed position) and could assume many positions: closed, so the audience saw a huge steel structure filling the width and height of the stage; open, so the colonnade units were flat to the wings with a large open playing space between them; and any spot between open and closed.

The units were human driven as opposed to motorized and could stop in any position and remain static until moved again. The actors were the engines of transition and set change, conceptually adding to the atmosphere of Coketown, which was crowded, always working, and dependent on the hard physical labor of the working-class inhabitants of the town. When the colonnades were in the open position, entrances and exits onto the upper levels of the colonnade could be made from offstage. With the colonnades in other positions, the upper level was entered by the actor climbing the rolling staircase or climbing the structure. Entrances and exits to the floor of the stage were dependent on the position of the colonnades: through the wings or through the arches.

Upstage of the colonnades was a nearly full-stage-sized painted scrim surrounded by a solid black frame. The colonnade units when open were flush to the frame. The scrim was painted as Coketown, with an industrial smoke- and smog-choked view of factories and smokestacks. Behind the scrim was another playing area, where the metaphoric circus and memory images appeared. The real circus scenes were played in front of the scrim, and the imagined circus scenes behind the scrim.

The set also included the rigged circus equipment, which could be flown in and out as needed, and a rolling staircase on free-floating castors, which could be placed anywhere on the stage and which allowed easy access to the second level of the colonnades. The lighting helped carve out the playing space of each scene; it was location specific and guided the transformations of the stage from scene to scene.

Although this specific design is not necessary to the production of the script, a reconception of the set should allow the kind of fluid and seamless transitions from one location to the next that this design made possible. The transitions between the various locations had an overlapping quality: characters and locations coalesced as previous ones faded. There was never a stopping of the story, never a blackout, which suited the episodic "meanwhile, back at Stone Lodge" kind of storytelling.

Hard Times

## CHARACTERS

Mr. Gradgrind

Mr. M'Choakumchild

Sissy

Louisa

Bitzer

Sleary

Tom

Bounderby

Mrs. Gradgrind

Amore

Kidderminster

Pufflerumpus

Mrs. Sparsit

Rachael

Stephen

Woman

Sissy's Mother

Sissy's Father

Mrs. Pegler

Harthouse

Slackbridge

*The play is set in the fictional city of Coketown,
northern England, in the 1850s.*

# ACT ONE

[*Music, the sounds of children laughing and playing, sounds of machinery and work. During the following barrage from* MR. GRAD-GRIND, *the scene morphs into a classroom.*]

## MURDERING THE INNOCENTS

MR. GRADGRIND:
I am Thomas Gradgrind, owner of this school. A man of fact and calculations. With a rule and a pair of scales, and the multiplication table always in his pocket, children, ready to weigh and measure any parcel of human nature, and tell you exactly what it comes to. Now, what I want is Facts. Teach these boys and girls nothing but Facts, Mr. M'Choakumchild!

MR. M'CHOAKUMCHILD:
Facts indeed, Mr. Gradgrind!

MR. GRADGRIND:

Facts alone are wanted in life. This is the principle on which I bring
up my own children, and this is the principle on which I bring up
these children. Stick to Facts! Girl Number Twenty, I don't know
that girl. Who is that girl?

SISSY:

Sissy Jupe, sir.

MR. GRADGRIND:

Sissy is not a name. Call yourself Cecilia.

SISSY:

It's Father as calls me Sissy, sir.

MR. GRADGRIND:

Tell him he mustn't. Cecilia Jupe. Let me see. What is your father?

SISSY:

He belongs to the circus, if you please, sir, he has an act with our
dog—

MR. GRADGRIND:

We don't want to know anything about that here. Your father
trains dogs, don't he? He doctors sick dogs, I dare say?

SISSY:

Oh yes, sir.

MR. GRADGRIND:

Very well, then. Describe him as a dog trainer and a veterinary sur-
geon. Give me your definition of a dog.

[SISSY *is thrown into great alarm by this demand.*]

MR. GRADGRIND:
Girl Number Twenty unable to define a dog! Girl Number Twenty possessed of no facts, in reference to one of the commonest of animals! Louisa, my own daughter, your definition.

LOUISA:
Quadruped. Omnivorous. Forty-two teeth. Skeletal frame consists of three hundred and nineteen bones. Sheds coat in the spring, Father! Sir.

MR. GRADGRIND:
Now, Girl Number Twenty, you know what a dog is. Let me ask you, girls and boys, would you paper a room with representations of dogs?

[*All say no except for* SISSY, *who says yes.*]

MR. GRADGRIND:
Of course, no. Bitzer, why not?

BITZER:
Sir, that would be ridiculous because dogs don't walk up and down the sides of rooms in reality, sir!

MR. GRADGRIND:
Very good Bitzer! You are a model student in this model school! Now, I'll try you children again. Suppose you were going to carpet a room. Would you use a carpet having a representation of flowers upon it?

*[All say no except for* SISSY, *who again says yes.]*

MR. GRADGRIND:
Girl Number Twenty! So you would carpet your room with representations of flowers, would you?

SISSY:
If you please, sir, I am very fond of flowers.

MR. GRADGRIND:
And is that why you would put tables and chairs upon them and have people walking over them with heavy boots?

SISSY:
It wouldn't hurt them, sir. They wouldn't crush and wither, if you please, sir. They would be the pictures of what was very pretty and pleasant, and I would fancy—

MR. GRADGRIND:
But you mustn't fancy. Fact, fact, fact! You don't walk upon flowers in fact; you cannot be allowed to walk upon flowers in carpets. Now, Mr. M'Choakumchild, I leave the children to you.

MR. M'CHOAKUMCHILD:
Thank you, Mr. Gradgrind, sir! We will be learning French, German, Latin, Greek, orthography, etymology, syntax and prosody, biography, astronomy, geography, and general cosmography, the sciences of compound proportion, algebra, land surveying, and leveling . . .

*[As the list drones on ("addition, subtraction, multiplication, divi-*

sion ..."), *the school bell rings. As the schoolhouse fades from view,*
*another scene coalesces.*]


## A LOOPHOLE

[*Music begins, and a circus barker appears.*]

SLEARY [*lisping*]:
Ladieth and thquireth, boyth and girlth, thith very afternoon Pro-
fethor Corneliuth Jupe will eluthidate the diverting accomplith-
menth of hith highly trained performing dog, Merrylegth—

[LOUISA *and* TOM *catch sight of the circus as they walk home from*
*school.*]

LOUISA:
Look Tom, a circus. . . .

TOM:
But what would Father say?

[*They peep in.*]

SLEARY:
Fraulein Pufflerumputh will inaugurate the entertainmenth with
her grathful rope-danthing act, Printh Don Carlo Amore will ex-
thibit hith athtounding featth of daring and death defianthe, and
lathtly but not leathtly, Mith Thitthy Jupe will fly through the air
on her thtupendouth cloud thwing! And now without further ado,
I give unto you, Thleary'th Thircuth!

[*The scene shifts to the inside of the circus where fabulous feats of*

*beauty, daring, and clowning are performed. The music and cos-*
*tumes are vibrant, fantastical, the very opposite of the world that's*
*been presented so far.* SISSY *is one of the performers. There is a*
*heightened moment as* LOUISA *watches* SISSY *fly through the air.*
LOUISA's *wonder, amazement, and longing emphasize the contrast*
*between the two girls. The routine ends, and the circus fades away*
*as* MR. GRADGRIND, *walking past on his way home, spots two stu-*
*dents watching.*]

MR. GRADGRIND:
Now, to think of these vagabonds attracting the young rabble from
a model school!

[*Outraged, he walks over to the two children.*]

Louisa! Thomas! My own children! In the name of wonder, idle-
ness, and folly! What do you do here?!

LOUISA:
Wanted to see what it was like.

MR. GRADGRIND:
Thomas, I find if difficult to believe that you, with your education
and resources, should have brought your sister to a scene like this.

LOUISA:
I brought him, Father. I asked him to come.

MR. GRADGRIND:
I am sorry to hear it. It makes Thomas no better, and it makes you
worse, Louisa. Thomas and you, who have been trained to mathe-
matical exactness! Here! In this degraded position! I am amazed.

LOUISA:
I was tired.

MR. GRADGRIND:
Tired? Of what?

LOUISA:
I don't know of what.

MR. GRADGRIND:
Say not another word. You are childish.

[*Music/transition.* MR. GRADGRIND *starts walking them home, perhaps a stylized walking in place.*]

MR. GRADGRIND [*walking*]:
What would your best friends say, Louisa? Do you attach no value to their good opinion? What would Mr. Bounderby say?

[MR. GRADGRIND *repeats these words under his breath as they walk home, and "home," Stone Lodge, morphs into being.*]

What would Mr. Bounderby say?

## MR. BOUNDERBY

[BOUNDERBY *and* MRS. GRADGRIND, *who is wheelchair bound, are at Stone Lodge in midconversation.*]

BOUNDERBY:
. . . I hadn't a shoe to my foot. As to a stocking, I didn't know such a thing by name. I passed the day in a ditch and the night in a

pigsty. That's the way I spent my tenth birthday. Not that a ditch was new to me, for I was born in a ditch.

MRS. GRADGRIND:
I hope it was a dry ditch, Mr. Bounderby?

BOUNDERBY:
A foot of water in it, Mrs. Gradgrind.

MRS. GRADGRIND:
Enough to give a baby cold. . . .

BOUNDERBY:
Cold? I was born with inflammation of the lungs, and of everything else that was capable of inflammation. For years, ma'am, I was one of the most miserable little wretches ever seen. I was so sickly that I was always moaning and groaning. I was so ragged and dirty that you wouldn't have touched me with a pair of tongs. How I fought through it, I don't know, but here I am, and nobody to thank for my being here but myself.

MRS. GRADGRIND:
Well, I hope your mother—

BOUNDERBY:
My mother? Bolted, ma'am. Left me to my grandmother who was the worst old woman that ever lived. If I got a little pair of shoes by any chance, she would take 'em off and sell 'em for drink. She kept me in an egg-box. That was the cot of my infancy, an old egg-box. As soon as I was big enough to run away, of course I ran away. I was to pull through it, I suppose, though nobody threw me out a rope. Banker and Mill Owner, ha, that would surprise my wicked

old grandmother! You may force me to swallow boiling fat, but you shall never force me to suppress the facts of my life!

[MR. GRADGRIND *and his two culprits come into the house.*]

MR. GRADGRIND [*with a nod to* BOUNDERBY]:
Mr. Bounderby.

BOUNDERBY:
Well, what's the matter? What are the children in the dumps about?

LOUISA:
We were peeping at the circus, and Father caught us.

MRS. GRADGRIND:
Louisa and Thomas! As if, with my head in its present throbbing state, you couldn't go and look at the shells and minerals and things provided for you instead of circuses! With my head in its present state, I couldn't remember the mere names of half the facts you have got to attend to.

LOUISA:
That's the reason.

MRS. GRADGRIND:
Don't tell me that's the reason, because it can be nothing of the sort. Wheel me into my room and go and be something-ological directly.

[*The children leave, wheeling* MRS. GRADGRIND.]

MR. GRADGRIND:

It appears that something has crept into Thomas's and Louisa's minds which I never intended to develop, and in which their reason has no part.

BOUNDERBY:

There certainly is no reason in looking with interest at a parcel of vagabonds. When I was a vagabond myself, nobody looked with any interest at me; I know that.

MR. GRADGRIND:

Then comes the question: In what has this vulgar curiosity its rise?

BOUNDERBY:

I'll tell you in what. In idle imagination.

MR. GRADGRIND:

That misgiving has crossed me on my way home.

BOUNDERBY:

In idle imagination, Gradgrind. A very bad thing for anybody, but a cursed bad thing for a girl like Louisa.

MR. GRADGRIND:

Whether any instructor or servant can have suggested anything? Whether, in spite of all precautions, any idle storybook can have got into the house? There is a girl from the circus in the school. . . .

BOUNDERBY:

Stop a bit! How did she come there?

MR. GRADGRIND:

Why, the fact is I saw the girl myself for the first time only just now.

BOUNDERBY:

Now, I tell you what, Gradgrind! Turn this girl out of your school, and there's an end of it.

MR. GRADGRIND:

I am much of your opinion.

BOUNDERBY:

"Do it at once" has always been my motto from a child. When I thought I would run away from my egg-box and my grandmother, I did it at once. Do you the same. Let's do this at once!

[*As they set off,* MR. GRADGRIND *leading the way,* BOUNDERBY *catches sight of* LOUISA *reentering the room. He stays back for a moment as* MR. GRADGRIND *leaves.*]

BOUNDERBY:

Louisa! It's all right, you won't be in any more trouble. I'll answer for it being all over with your father. Well, Louisa, that's worth a kiss, isn't it?

LOUISA:

You can take one, Mr. Bounderby.

[*She stands very still and, when* BOUNDERBY *approaches, raises her cheek to him, her face turned away.*]

BOUNDERBY [*with a kiss*]:
Always my pet, a'n't you, Louisa? Good-bye, Louisa.

[*Music/transition.* BOUNDERBY *leaves and trots to catch up with* MR. GRADGRIND. LOUISA *stands on the same spot rubbing and rubbing her cheek where he kissed her. As the focus shifts to* MR. GRADGRIND *and* BOUNDERBY, LOUISA *continues rubbing.*]

## SLEARY'S CIRCUS

[BOUNDERBY *and* MR. GRADGRIND *walk to the circus. On their way they come across* SISSY, *who is running in the direction in which they are walking.*]

MR. GRADGRIND:
Hallo! Stop! Where are you going, Girl Number Twenty?

[SISSY *pulls up.*]

SISSY:
Home, sir.

MR. GRADGRIND:
We are going there as well, girl. Take us to your father.

[*They walk. City street noises pick up as they move toward the poorer neighborhoods.*]

What have you got in that bottle you are carrying?

BOUNDERBY:
Gin.

SISSY:
Oh, no, sir! It's the nine oils.

BOUNDERBY:
The what oils?

SISSY:
The nine oils, sir. To rub Father with.

BOUNDERBY:
What the devil do you rub your father with nine oils for?

SISSY:
It's what our people always use, sir, when they get any hurts in the ring. They bruise themselves very bad sometimes.

BOUNDERBY:
Serves 'em right for being idle. By George! When I was four or five years younger than you, I had worse bruises upon me than ten oils, twenty oils, forty oils would have rubbed off. I didn't get 'em by posture making but by being banged about!

[*A new location has morphed around them. Two circus performers, on break from performing, loiter nearby.*]

SISSY [*to the* CIRCUS FOLK]:
They're here for Father. [*To* MR. GRADGRIND] Here we are, sir.

[SISSY *goes inside, followed by* BOUNDERBY *and* MR. GRADGRIND.]

If you should hear a dog, sir, it's only Merrylegs, and he only barks. Father? . . . Father? . . . That's strange—he doesn't seem to be here.

BOUNDERBY:
Merrylegs and nine oils, eh!

[SISSY *opens a trunk and looks in.*]

SISSY:
Why, all his things are gone. . . . Father must have gone down to the Pegasus's Arms, sir. I don't know why he should go there, but he must be there; I'll bring him in a minute!

[SISSY *runs off.*]

MR. GRADGRIND:
What does she mean! Back in a minute? It's more than a mile off.

[AMORE *and* KIDDERMINSTER *enter the room dressed in a "between-shows" form of their circus costumes (shabby robe over glittering costume, etc.).*]

AMORE:
You were looking for Señor Jupe?

MR. GRADGRIND:
I am. His daughter has gone to fetch him, but I can't wait; therefore, if you please, I will leave a message for him with you.

BOUNDERBY:
You see, my friend, we are the kind of people who know the value of time, and you are the kind of people who don't know the value of time.

AMORE:

If you mean that you can make more money of your time than I can of mine, I should judge from your appearance that you are about right.

KIDDERMINSTER:

Tick-tock, Governor, time's a-wasting. . . .

AMORE:

Kidderminster, stow that!

KIDDERMINSTER:

What does he come here cheeking us for, then? If you want to cheek us, pay your ochre at the door.

AMORE:

Kidderminster, stow that! [To MR. GRADGRIND] Sir, you may or you may not be aware that Jupe has missed his tip very often lately.

MR. GRADGRIND:

Has—what has he missed?

AMORE:

Missed his tip.

KIDDERMINSTER:

Missed his tip at the banners and was loose in his ponging, too—

AMORE:

Didn't do what he ought to do. Was short in his leaps and bad in his tumbling.

MR. GRADGRIND:
Oh! That is tip, is it?

AMORE:
In a general way that's missing his tip.

BOUNDERBY:
Nine oils, Merrylegs, missing tips, banners, and ponging, eh! Queer sort of company, too, for a man who has raised himself!

KIDDERMINSTER:
Lower yourself, then. Oh, Lord! If you've raised yourself so high as all that comes to, let yourself down a bit.

MR. GRADGRIND:
This is a very obtrusive lad!

KIDDERMINSTER:
We'd have had the king of England to meet you, if only we had known you were coming.

[AMORE *stares down* KIDDERMINSTER, *who goes out and sits on the steps.*]

AMORE:
Forgive me. You were going to give me a message for Jupe?

MR. GRADGRIND:
Yes, I was—

AMORE:
Then my opinion is he will never receive it. Do you know much of him?

MR. GRADGRIND:

I never saw the man in my life.

AMORE:

I doubt if you ever will see him now. It's pretty plain to me, he's off.

MR. GRADGRIND:

Do you mean that he has deserted his daughter?

AMORE:

Aye! He was goosed last night, he was goosed the night before last, he was goosed today. He has lately got in the way of being always goosed, and he can't stand it.

MR. GRADGRIND:

Why has he been . . . so very much . . . Goosed?

AMORE:

His joints are turning stiff, and he is getting used up. Now, it's a re-markable fact, sir, that it cut that man deeper to know that his daughter knew of his being goosed than to go through with it.

BOUNDERBY:

Good! This is good, Gradgrind! A man so fond of his daughter that he runs away from her! This is devilish good! Ha ha! Now, I'll tell you what, young man. I haven't always occupied my present sta-tion of life. You may be astonished to hear it, but my mother ran away from me.

AMORE:

This astonishes me? No, it does not. [To MR. GRADGRIND] Jupe sent his daughter out on an errand not an hour ago and then was seen to slip out himself, with his hat over his eyes and a bundle tied up in a handkerchief under his arm. She will never believe it of him, but he has cut away and left her.

MR. GRADGRIND:
Pray, why will she never believe it of him?

AMORE:
Because, up to this time, he seemed to dote upon her. Poor Sissy! Her father always had it in his head that she was to be educated. When Sissy got into your school, he was very pleased. If you should happen to have looked in tonight, for the purpose of telling him that you were going to do her any little service, it would be very fortunate and well timed.

MR. GRADGRIND:
On the contrary, I came to tell him that she must not attend the school anymore. Still, if her father really has left her, without any connivance on her part—Bounderby, may I have a word with you?

[SLEARY *and* PUFFLERUMPUS *arrive.* KIDDERMINSTER *and* AMORE *have a quick word with* SLEARY, *and they all end up in the room.*]

SLEARY:
Thquire! Your thervant! Thith ith a bad piethe of bithnith, thith ith. You've heard of my runaway clown, Thithy'th father, and hith dog being thuppothed to have morrithed?

MR. GRADGRIND:
Yes.

SLEARY:
Well, Thquire, ith it your intenthion to do anything for the poor girl, Thquire?

MR. GRADGRIND:
I shall have something to propose to her when she comes back.

SLEARY:
Glad to hear it, Thquire. Not that I want to get rid of the child, any more than I want to thtand in her way—

[SISSY *runs into the room. When she sees them all there, sees their faces, and sees no father, she bursts into tears.*]

Ith an infernal thame, upon my thoul it ith.

SISSY:
Oh, Father, Father. . . .

[*All stand around not quite knowing what to do.*]

BOUNDERBY:
Your father has absconded—deserted you—and you mustn't expect to see him again as long as you live.

[*The* CIRCUS FOLK *are upset and lunge for* BOUNDERBY. SLEARY *holds them back.*]

SLEARY:
I tell you what, Thquire. Thethe are a very good natur'd people, but they're accuthtomed to be quick in their movementh; and if you don't cut it thort and drop it, I'm damned if I don't believe they'll pith you out o' winder.

MR. GRADGRIND:

I came here for a different reason but am prepared in these altered circumstances to make a proposal. I am willing to take charge of you, Jupe, and to educate you and provide for you. The only condition I make is that you decide at once whether to accompany me or remain here.

SLEARY:

If you like, Thethilia, to thtay, you know the nature of the work and you know your companionth.

MR. GRADGRIND:

The only observation I will make to you, Jupe, is that it is highly desirable to have a sound practical education and that even your father himself appears, on your behalf, to have known and felt that much.

[*This catches* SISSY'*s attention. She stops crying and looks fully on* MR. GRADGRIND. *Silence.*]

SISSY:

When Father comes back, how will he find me if I go away!

MR. GRADGRIND:

You may be quite at ease, Jupe, on that score. In such a case, your father must find out Mr. . . .

SLEARY:

Thleary. That'th my name, Thquire. Not athamed of it. Known all over England, and alwayth paythe ith way.

MR. GRADGRIND:

. . . must find out Mr. Sleary, who would then let him know where you went. I should have no power of keeping you against his wish, and he would have no difficulty in finding Mr. Thomas Gradgrind of Coketown.

[*Silence.*]

SISSY:
Oh, give me my clothes, give me my clothes, and let me go away before I break my heart!

[*They give* MR. GRADGRIND *the trunk.*]

MR. GRADGRIND:
Now, Jupe, if you are quite determined, come!

[SLEARY *hugs her.*]

SLEARY:
Leave the bottle, my dear; it'th large to carry; it will be of no uthe to you now.

SISSY:
No, no! Let me keep it for Father till he comes back! I must keep it for him, in case he has some hurts when he comes back to get me!

SLEARY:
Tho be it, my dear. Farewell, thweet Thethelia! My latht wordth to you ith thisth: Thtick to the termth of your engagement, be obedient to the thquire, and forget uth. But if, when you're grown up and married and well off, you come upon any thircuth ever, don't be hard upon it, don't be croth with it, and think you might do wurth. People mutht be amuthed, Thquire, thomehow . . . they

can't be alwayth a-working, nor yet they can't be alwayth a-learning. Make the betht of uth, not the wurtht.

[*Music/transition. As* MR. GRADGRIND, BOUNDERBY, *and* SISSY *leave,*
SISSY *hugs and says good-bye to the* CIRCUS FOLK. *Once outside
the room,* BOUNDERBY *parts company while* SISSY *and* MR. GRAD-
GRIND *return to Stone Lodge.* LOUISA *is where we left her (perhaps
we never left her), with her hand still on the spot where* BOUND-
ERBY *kissed her. The focus shifts to the scene at Stone Lodge.*]

MR. GRADGRIND:
Mrs. Gradgrind, Thomas, Louisa, your presence is requested.

[MRS. GRADGRIND *and* THOMAS *appear and join* LOUISA.]

This is Cecilia Jupe, former circus girl. Her father has left her and
her mother is dead and I have made up my mind to take her into
our house.

MRS. GRADGRIND:
Oh my . . . I feel quite light-headed. . . .

MR. GRADGRIND:
Jupe, this is Thomas and Louisa. When you are not in attendance
at the school, I will employ you about Mrs. Gradgrind, who is
rather an invalid. The whole subject of your late career is past and
is not to be referred to anymore. From this time you begin your
history. You are, at present, ignorant, I know.

SISSY:
Yes, sir, very.

MR. GRADGRIND:

I shall have the satisfaction of causing you to be strictly educated, and you will be a living proof to all who come into communication with you of the advantages of the training you will receive. Do you read?

SISSY:

Only to Father and Merrylegs, sir.

MR. GRADGRIND:

Never mind Merrylegs, Jupe. I don't ask about the dog. So you have been in the habit of reading to your father?

SISSY:

Oh yes, sir, thousands of times.

MR. GRADGRIND:

And what did you read to your father, Jupe?

SISSY:

About the fairies, the dwarf, the hunchback, the genies—

MR. GRADGRIND:

Hush! Never breathe a word of such destructive nonsense anymore. Louisa, make up a bed for Jupe; she has had a difficult day and must be tired.

[*Music/transition.*]


## MRS. SPARSIT

[*A room at* BOUNDERBY's *house.*]

MRS. SPARSIT:
Mr. Bounderby, you are unusually slow, sir, with your tea this evening.

BOUNDERBY:
Why, Mrs. Sparsit, I am thinking about Tom Gradgrind's whim of bringing up the tumbling girl. His whim of letting her have an association with Louisa.

MRS. SPARSIT:
Indeed, Mr. Bounderby? Very thoughtful of you!

BOUNDERBY:
It's tolerably clear to me that the little puss can get small good out of such companionship.

MRS. SPARSIT:
Are you speaking of young Miss Gradgrind, Mr. Bounderby?

BOUNDERBY:
Yes, ma'am, I am speaking of Louisa.

MRS. SPARSIT:
Your observation being limited to "little puss" and there being two little girls in question, I did not know which might be indicated by that expression.

BOUNDERBY:
Louisa, Louisa, Louisa.

MRS. SPARSIT:
You are quite another father to Louisa, sir.

[BOUNDERBY *chokes a little on his tea.*]

BOUNDERBY:
No, no, I'm another father to Tom. I am going to take young Tom into my office, have him live here, have him under my wing! But here I am speaking to you this evening about tumblers! Why, what do you know about tumblers? At the time when to have been a tumbler in the mud of the streets would have been a godsend to me, a prize in the lottery to me, you were at the Italian Opera. And now you work for me.

MRS. SPARSIT:
I certainly, sir, was familiar with Italian Opera at a very early age.

BOUNDERBY:
Egad, ma'am, so was I. With the wrong side of it. A hard bed the pavement of its arcade used to make, I assure you. People like you, ma'am, accustomed from infancy to lie on down feathers, have no idea how hard a paving stone is without trying it.

MRS. SPARSIT:
How true, sir, and if I have acquired an interest in hearing of your instructive experiences, and can scarcely hear enough of them, I claim no merit for that, since I believe it is a general sentiment.

BOUNDERBY:
Well, ma'am, perhaps some people may be pleased to say that they do like to hear, in his own unpolished way, what Josiah Bounderby of Coketown has gone through. But you must confess that you were born in the lap of luxury yourself. Come, ma'am, you know you were born in the lap of luxury.

MRS. SPARSIT:
I do not, sir, deny it.

BOUNDERBY:
And you were in crack society. Devilish high society.

MRS. SPARSIT:
It is true, sir.

BOUNDERBY:
You were in the tip-top fashion, and all the rest of it.

MRS. SPARSIT:
Yes, sir, it is unquestionably true.

BOUNDERBY:
You have come down in the world and I have come up, up, up!

[*Music/transition. A sequence of images: the children at school and the workers in the mills, all moving with mechanized, repetitive actions. Highlighted in this sequence are the two mill workers,* RACHAEL *and* STEPHEN.]


NEVER WONDER

[*At the Gradgrinds' home, Stone Lodge.* TOM *and* LOUISA *sit staring into the fireplace in a twilit room.*]

TOM:
I am sick of my life, Loo. I hate it altogether, and I hate everybody except you.

LOUISA:
You don't hate Sissy, Tom?

TOM:
She hates me.

LOUISA:
No she does not, Tom.

TOM:
She must just hate and detest the whole setout of us. As to me, I am a Donkey, that's what I am. I am as obstinate as one, I am more stupid than one, and I should like to kick like one.

LOUISA:
Not me, I hope, Tom?

TOM:
No, Loo; I wouldn't hurt you. I don't know what this jolly old Jaundiced Jail would be without you.

LOUISA:
But Tom, I don't know what other girls know. I can't play to you, or sing to you. I can't talk to you so as to lighten your mind, for I never see any amusing sights or read any amusing books.

TOM:
Well, no more do I. I am as bad as you in that respect.

LOUISA:
It's very unfortunate for both of us.

TOM:

Oh! You, you are a girl, Loo, and a girl comes out of it better than a boy does. I don't miss anything in you. You can brighten even this place—and you can always lead me as you like.

LOUISA:

You are a dear brother, Tom.

[LOUISA *goes to kiss him, then returns to staring at the fire.*]

TOM:

I wish I could collect all the Facts we hear so much about and all the Figures, and all the people who found them out; and I wish I could put a thousand barrels of gunpowder under them, and blow them all up together! However, when I go to live with old Bounderby, I'll have my revenge.

LOUISA:

Your revenge, Tom?

TOM:

I mean, I'll enjoy myself a little, and go about and see something, and hear something. I'll recompense myself for the way in which I have been brought up.

LOUISA:

But don't disappoint yourself beforehand, Tom. Mr. Bounderby thinks as Father thinks and is a great deal rougher and not half so kind.

TOM [*laughing*]:

Oh, I don't mind that. I shall very well know how to manage and smooth old Bounderby!

LOUISA:
How, Tom? Is it a secret?

TOM:
It's you. You are his favorite; he'll do anything for you. When he says to me what I don't like, I shall say to him, "My sister Loo will be hurt and disappointed, Mr. Bounderby. She always used to tell me she was sure you would be easier with me than this."

[LOUISA *is silent for a long while.*]

TOM:
Have you gone to sleep, Loo?

LOUISA:
No, Tom. I am looking at the fire.

TOM:
You seem to find more to look at in it than ever I could find.

LOUISA:
Tom, do you look forward with any satisfaction to this change to Mr. Bounderby's?

TOM:
Why, there's one thing to be said of it; it will be getting away from home.

LOUISA:
It will be getting away from home. Yes.

TOM:

I must go, you know, whether I like it or not; and I had better go where I can take with me some advantage of your influence than where I should lose it altogether, don't you see?

LOUISA [*pausing, staring into the fire*]:
Yes, Tom.

[TOM *goes to look at the fire from her point of view to see what he can make of it. Music begins and plays under the next bit.*]

TOM:

Except that it is a fire it looks to me as stupid and blank as everything else looks. What do you see in it?

[*The scene pauses here, with* TOM *leaning over* LOUISA, *arms on the back of her chair, looking at the fire. What* LOUISA *sees in the fire appears: a circus routine with* SISSY *high in the air. The free, beautiful, and emotional image of* SISSY *contrasts sharply with the still, blank, marble* LOUISA.]

TOM:
What do you see, Loo?

LOUISA:
Nothing, Tom. Nothing but what's there.


## STEPHEN BLACKPOOL

[*In the mill. The end-of-day whistle sounds, and the mill workers close down their looms and begin to leave.* STEPHEN BLACKPOOL *catches* RACHAEL.]

STEPHEN:

Rachael! I looked for you last night for to walk you home.

RACHAEL:

'Times I'm a little early, Stephen, 'times a little late. I'm never to be counted on, going home.

STEPHEN:

Not going the other way either, it seems to me, Rachael?

RACHAEL:

No, Stephen. We are such true friends, lad, and such old friends, and getting to be such old folk, now—

STEPHEN:

No, Rachael, thou art as young as ever thou was.

RACHAEL:

One of us would be puzzled how to get old, Stephen, without the other getting so, too, both being alive. . . . But anyways, we're such old friends that to hide a word of honest truth from one another would be a sin and a pity. 'Tis better not to walk too much together. Sometimes, yes! It would be hard, indeed, if it was not to be at all.

STEPHEN:

'Tis hard anyways, Rachael.

RACHAEL:

Try to think not, and it will seem better.

STEPHEN:

I've tried a long time, and it hasn't got better. But thou art right; it might make folk talk, even of thee. Thou hast done me so much good, Rachael, that thy word is a law to me, and a bright good law! Better than some real ones.

RACHAEL:
Let the laws be.

STEPHEN:
Yes. Let 'em be. Let everything be. Let all sorts alone. 'Tis a muddle, and that's all.

RACHAEL [smiling]:
Always a muddle?

STEPHEN [laughing]:
Aye, Rachael, lass, always a muddle. That's where I stick. I come to the muddle many times and again, and I never get beyond it.

STEPHEN:
Good night, dear lass, good night!

RACHAEL:
Good night.

[They part. STEPHEN walks to his cramped and tiny home, lights a candle, and sees something on the floor. It is a WOMAN, a stumbling drunk.]

STEPHEN:
Heaven's mercy, woman! Hast thou come back again!

WOMAN:
Back again? Yes! And back again. Back again ever and ever so of-

ten. Back? Yes, back. Why not? I'll sell off all your things again, and I'll sell thee off again, and I'll sell thee off a score of times, what's yours is mine, that's what ye promised long ago!

[STEPHEN *sits on the bed, head in his hands.*]

WOMAN:
Come away from the bed! Come away from it. 'Tis mine, and I've a right to it!

[*The* WOMAN *falls onto the bed.* STEPHEN *lies down on the floor. Night passes in Coketown. Music/transition.* STEPHEN'*s house fades as the focus goes to a room in Stone Lodge.*]


## SISSY'S PROGRESS

[SISSY *and* LOUISA *are studying in Stone Lodge, the Gradgrinds' home.*]

SISSY:
It would be a fine thing to be you, Miss Louisa!

LOUISA:
Do you think so?

SISSY:
I should know so much, Miss Louisa. All that is difficult to me now would be so easy then.

LOUISA:
You might not be the better for it, Sissy. You are more useful to my mother and more pleasant with her than I could ever be. . . .

SISSY:

But I am oh so stupid! All through school hours I make mistakes. I can't help them. They seem to come natural to me.

LOUISA:

And the teachers never make any mistakes themselves, I suppose, Sissy?

[*An image of* MR. M'CHOAKUMCHILD *is conjured.*]

SISSY:

Oh no! They know everything.

MR. M'CHOAKUMCHILD:

I know everything.

LOUISA:

Tell me some of your mistakes.

SISSY:

I am almost ashamed. But today, for instance, Mr. M'Choakumchild was explaining to us about . . .

MR. M'CHOAKUMCHILD:

. . . natural prosperity . . .

LOUISA:

"National," I think it must have been.

SISSY:

Yes, it was. But isn't it the same?

LOUISA:
You had better say "National," as he said so.

SISSY/MR. M'CHOAKUMCHILD [MR. M'CHOAKUMCHILD *shaking his head confusedly at his previous malapropism*]:
National Prosperity . . .

SISSY:
And he said:

MR. M'CHOAKUMCHILD:
Now, this schoolroom is a Nation. And in this nation, there are fifty millions of money. Isn't this a prosperous nation? Girl Number Twenty, isn't this a prosperous nation, and a'n't you in a thriving state?

SISSY [*to* MR. M'CHOAKUMCHILD]:
I can't know whether it is a prosperous nation or not, and whether I am in a thriving state or not, unless I know who has got the money, and whether any of it is mine.

LOUISA:
That was a great mistake of yours.

SISSY:
It was not in the figures at all. . . .

MR. M'CHOAKUMCHILD:
Girl Number Twenty, I'll try you again. This schoolroom is an immense town, and in it there are a million of inhabitants, and only five-and-twenty are starved to death in the streets in the course of a year. What is your remark on that proportion?

SISSY:

I think it must be just as hard upon those who are starved, whether the others are a million, or a million million.

LOUISA:

And that was wrong, too.

MR. M'CHOAKUMCHILD:

I'll try you once more. Here are the stutterings . . .

LOUISA:

Statistics.

SISSY:

Yes, Miss Louisa—they always remind me of stuttering, and that's another of my mistakes . . .

MR. M'CHOAKUMCHILD [*again shaking his head*]:

. . . statistics of accidents upon the sea. And I find that in a given time a hundred thousand persons went to sea on long voyages, and only five hundred of them were drowned or burnt to death. What is the percentage?

SISSY:

One hundred percent.

LOUISA:

One hundred percent?

MR. M'CHOAKUMCHILD:

One hundred percent?

SISSY:
One hundred percent, master—to the relations and friends of the people who were killed.

MR. M'CHOAKUMCHILD:
Wrong, wrong, wrong!

[*The image of* MR. M'CHOAKUMCHILD *fades.*]

SISSY:
I shall never learn. And the worst of all is that, although my poor father wished me so much to learn, I am afraid I don't like it.

LOUISA:
Did your father know so much himself that he wished you to be well taught, too, Sissy?

[SISSY *hesitates.*]

No one hears us; and if anyone did, I am sure no harm could be found in such an innocent question.

SISSY:
No, Miss Louisa, Father knows very little indeed.

LOUISA:
Your mother?

SISSY:
Father says she was quite a scholar. She died when I was born. She was . . . she was a rope dancer.

[*Music. An image is conjured of* SISSY'S MOTHER *and* SISSY'S FA-
THER, *a circus routine that plays "under" the next bit of scene.*
SISSY'S MOTHER *rope dances in an "Arabian Nights"-style outfit to
echo the reference to Scherezade coming up.* SISSY'S FATHER *is
dressed as a clown and assists with the routine.*]

LOUISA:
Did your father love her?

SISSY:
Oh yes! As dearly as he loves me.

LOUISA:
Where did you live?

SISSY:
We traveled about the country and had no fixed place to live in. Father's a [*whispering*] . . . a clown.

LOUISA [*nodding*]:
To make the people laugh?

SISSY:
Yes. But they wouldn't laugh sometimes, and then Father cried.

LOUISA:
And you were his comfort through everything?

SISSY:
Father said I was. I used to read to him to cheer his courage, and he
was very fond of that. They were wrong books—I am never to
speak of them here—but we didn't know there was any harm in
them.

40

LOUISA:

And he liked them?


SISSY:

Oh, very much! And often and often of a night, he used to forget all his troubles in wondering whether the sultan would let the lady go on with the story or would have her head cut off before it was finished.


LOUISA:

And your father was always kind?


SISSY:

He was so kind to me and Merrylegs. [*Whispering*] Merrylegs is his performing dog.


LOUISA:

Finish by telling me how your father left you, Sissy. Now that I have asked you so much, tell me the end.


SISSY:

Dear Miss Louisa, I came home from the circus that afternoon, and found poor Father just come home, too.


[LOUISA *watches the action.* SISSY'S FATHER, *dressed as a clown, sits on the ground, rocking himself as if in pain.*]


SISSY:

Have you hurt yourself, Father?


[SISSY'S FATHER *hides his face, his body shaking with sobs.*]

SISSY'S FATHER:
My darling! My love! Oh, I am a shame and a disgrace! A clown
who can't make people laugh . . . you would have done better without me. . . .

SISSY:
But, Father, I think you're very funny . . . please don't cry. . . .

[SISSY'S FATHER *gets himself under better control.*]

SISSY'S FATHER:
Tell me about your school, my dear Sissy. . . .

SISSY:
Well, today we learned about dogs and rugs and wallpaper and
some other facts, Father.

SISSY'S FATHER:
That's good, Sissy. I want so badly for you to know a great deal. . . .
I want so badly for you to be different from me. . . . I need you to
fetch me some nine oils for the little hurt I have, my darling.

[SISSY *is reluctant to go.*]

SISSY:
Father, dear, shall I take Merrylegs?

SISSY'S FATHER:
No, Sissy, no; take nothing that's known to be mine, my darling. . . .

[SISSY *reaches out to him as his image fades away.*]

SISSY [to LOUISA]:
When I came back, he was gone. I keep the nine oils ready for him, and I know he will come back. Every letter that I see in Mr. Gradgrind's hand takes my breath away and blinds my eyes, for I think it comes from Father. . . .

[MR. GRADGRIND appears. He is carrying mail.]

I beg your pardon, sir, for being a bother—but . . . do you have a letter yet from Father?

MR. GRADGRIND:
No, Jupe, nothing of the sort.


## NO WAY OUT

[Music/transition. STEPHEN is walking down a street. He knocks on a door that opens onto BOUNDERBY's giant hall, where BOUND-ERBY sits at a large table, eating.]

BOUNDERBY:
Now, Stephen Blackpool, you have never been one of my unreasonable Hands. You don't expect to be fed on turtle soup and venison with a gold spoon, as a good many of 'em do, and therefore I know already that you have not come here to make a complaint.

STEPHEN:
No, sir, sure I have not come for nothing of the kind.

BOUNDERBY:
Very well, fire away!

STEPHEN:

I were married on Easter Monday nineteen year ago. She were a young lass with good accounts of herself. Well, she went bad— soon. Not along of me. God knows I were not an unkind husband to her.

BOUNDERBY:

I have heard all this before. She took to drinking, left off working, sold the furniture, pawned the clothes, and played old Gooseberry.

STEPHEN:

I were patient with her. I tried to wean her from it, over and over again. Finally, I paid her to keep away from me. These five year I have paid her. Last night, I went home. There she lay upon my hearthstone! There she is!

BOUNDERBY:

It's a bad job; that's what it is. You had better have been satisfied as you were, and not have got married. However, it's too late to say that.

MRS. SPARSIT:

Was it an unequal marriage, sir, in point of years?

[BOUNDERBY *coughs, choking on some food.*]

BOUNDERBY:

You hear what this lady asks. Was it an unequal marriage in point of years, this unlucky job of yours?

STEPHEN:

Not even so. I were one-and-twenty myself; she were twenty.

MRS. SPARSIT:
Indeed, sir? I inferred, from its being so miserable a marriage, that it was probably an unequal one in point of years.

[BOUNDERBY *takes a drink.*]

BOUNDERBY:
Well? Why don't you go on?

STEPHEN:
I have come to ask you, sir, how I am to be ridded of this woman. I cannot bear it no more. I have lived under it so long, because I have had the pity and comforting words of the best lass living or dead.

MRS. SPARSIT:
He wishes to be free, to marry the female of whom he speaks, I fear, sir.

STEPHEN:
I were a-coming to it. I have read in the papers that great folk are not bonded together for better for worse so fast but that they can be set free from their misfortunate marriages, and marry over again, and I want to know how.

BOUNDERBY:
No how.

STEPHEN:
If I do her any hurt, sir, there's a law to punish me?

BOUNDERBY:
Of course there is.

STEPHEN:
If I flee from her, there's a law to punish me?

BOUNDERBY:
Of course there is.

STEPHEN:
If I marry the other dear lass, there's a law to punish me?

BOUNDERBY:
Of course there is.

STEPHEN:
Now, in God's name, show me the law to help me!

BOUNDERBY:
There is such a law, but it's not for you at all. Why, you'd have to get an Act of Parliament to enable you to marry again, and it would cost you, I suppose, from a thousand to fifteen hundred pound!

STEPHEN:
There's no other law?

BOUNDERBY:
Certainly not.

STEPHEN:
Why then, sir, 'tis a muddle. 'Tis just a muddle altogether, and the sooner I am dead, the better.

BOUNDERBY:
Pooh, pooh! Don't you call the Institutions of your country a muddle. You didn't take your wife for fast and for loose, but for better

for worse. If she has turned out worse—why, all we have got to say is she might have turned out better.

STEPHEN:
'Tis a muddle.

BOUNDERBY:
Now, you have always been a steady Hand hitherto, but my opinion is that you are turning into the wrong road. You have been listening to some mischievous stranger or other—they're always about—and the best thing you can do is to come out of that.

STEPHEN:
Thank you, sir, good evening, sir.

[STEPHEN *is back out on the street, where he is approached by an* OLD WOMAN.]


## THE OLD WOMAN

OLD WOMAN:
Pray, sir, didn't I see you come out of that gentleman's house?

STEPHEN:
Yes, missus.

OLD WOMAN:
Have you—you'll excuse an old woman's curiosity—have you seen the gentleman?

STEPHEN:
Yes, missus.

OLD WOMAN:

And how did he look, sir? Was he portly, bold, outspoken, and hearty?

STEPHEN:

Oh yes, he were all that.

OLD WOMAN:

And healthy as the fresh wind?

STEPHEN:

Yes. He were eating and drinking—as large and as loud as a Hummobee.

OLD WOMAN:

Aye, that be him! Thank you! Thank you!

[STEPHEN *starts to leave.*]

I come by the train. Once a year. I spend my savings so, once every year. I come regular, to tramp about the streets and see my gentleman.

STEPHEN:

Only to see him?

OLD WOMAN:

That's enough for me. I ask no more! But he's late this year, and I have not seen him. You came out, instead. Now, if I am obliged to go back without a glimpse of him, well, I have seen you, and you have seen him, and I must make that do. Had you business with the fine gentleman?

hear that Mr. Bounderby is taking you on at the bank as an assistant to young Tom. Continue to work hard, young man.

BITZER:
Thank you, Headmaster!

[*He shakes* BITZER'*s hand, takes his slate, and* BITZER *moves to his tiny new desk at the bank and begins working as* MR. GRADGRIND *moves on to* SISSY.]

MR. GRADGRIND:
I fear, Jupe, that your continuance at the school any longer would be useless.

SISSY:
I am afraid it would, sir.

MR. GRADGRIND:
I cannot disguise from you, Jupe, my disappointment. You have not acquired the knowledge which I looked for. You are extremely deficient in your facts. Your acquaintance with figures is very limited. You are altogether backward, and below the mark.

SISSY:
I am sorry, sir, yet I have tried hard.

MR. GRADGRIND:
Yes, I have observed you, and I can find no fault in that respect.

SISSY:
I have thought sometimes that perhaps I tried to learn too much, and that if I had asked to be allowed to try a little less, I might have—

MR. GRADGRIND:

No, Jupe, no. The course you pursued, you pursued according to the system, and there is no more to be said about it.

SISSY:

Oh, Mr. Gradgrind, you've been so kind to me. . . . I wish I could have done better for you—

MR. GRADGRIND:

Don't shed tears, don't shed tears. I don't complain of you. You are an affectionate, earnest, good young woman, and—and we must make that do.

SISSY:

Thank you very much, sir.

MR. GRADGRIND:

You are useful to Mrs. Gradgrind, and you are serviceable in the family also. Now that I've been elected to Parliament and will be much in London, your presence in the household will be rather appreciated. I hope you can be happy with that.

SISSY:

I should have nothing to wish, sir, if—

MR. GRADGRIND:

You refer to your father. I have heard from Miss Louisa that you still preserve that bottle. Well, if your training in the science of arriving at exact results had been more successful, you would have been wiser on these points. I will say no more. Good night, Jupe.

SISSY:
Good night.

[*Music as* TOM *dumps his huge pile of work on* BITZER's *desk and comes to Stone Lodge. He looks in the room where* LOUISA *is sitting, staring at the fire.*]

TOM:
Are you there, Loo?

LOUISA:
Dear Tom, how long it is since you have been to see me!

TOM:
Why, I have been otherwise engaged, Loo, in the evenings; and in the daytime old Bounderby has been keeping me at it rather. But I touch him up with you when he comes it too strong, and so we preserve an understanding. Has Father said anything particular to you, today or yesterday, Loo?

LOUISA:
No, Tom. But he told me he wished to do so tonight.

TOM:
Ahh. Do you know where he is?

LOUISA:
No.

TOM:
He's with old Bounderby. They are having a regular confab together, up at the bank. I'll bet you a hundred pounds that I know what it's about!

[LOUISA *stares at the fire.* TOM *encircles her waist with his arm and draws her to him.*]

TOM:
You are very fond of me, a'n't you, Loo?

LOUISA:
Indeed I am, Tom, though you do let such long intervals go by without coming to see me.

TOM:
Well, sister of mine, when you say that, you are near my thoughts. We might be so much oftener together. Always together, almost. It would do me a great deal of good if you were to make up your mind to I know what, Loo. It would be uncommonly jolly!

[*He looks hard at her and kisses her cheek.*]

I can't stay because I'm engaged to some fellows tonight. You won't forget how fond you are of me?

LOUISA:
No, dear Tom, I won't forget.

TOM:
That's a capital girl. Good-bye, Loo.


## HUSBAND AND WIFE

[*Music. At* BOUNDERBY'S *house,* BOUNDERBY *and* MR. GRADGRIND *shake hands, then* MR. GRADGRIND *leaves.* BOUNDERBY *is about to enter his room at home, where* MRS. SPARSIT *is sitting and knitting, but before he goes in, he takes a vial from his pocket, unstops it, puts it to his nose, and reacts violently.*]

BOUNDERBY:
By George, if she takes it in a fainting way, I'll have the skin off her nose!

[BOUNDERBY *enters nervously.*]

MRS. SPARSIT:
Good evening, Mr. Bounderby!

BOUNDERBY:
Good evening, ma'am, good evening.

[MRS. SPARSIT *draws her chair back.*]

BOUNDERBY:
Don't go to the North Pole, ma'am!

MRS. SPARSIT:
Thank you, sir.

[*She returns her seat, although short of its former position.* BOUNDERBY *looks at* MRS. SPARSIT; *she works on her knitting.*]

BOUNDERBY:
Mrs. Sparsit, ma'am, I am going to astonish you.

MRS. SPARSIT [*tranquilly, putting down her work and attending*]:
Yes, sir?

BOUNDERBY:
I am going, ma'am, to marry Tom Gradgrind's daughter.

MRS. SPARSIT:
Yes, sir? I hope you may be happy, Mr. Bounderby. Oh, indeed I hope you may be happy, sir! I wish with all my heart, sir, that you may be in all respects very happy.

BOUNDERBY:
Well, ma'am, I am obliged to you. I hope I shall be.

MRS. SPARSIT:
*Do* you, sir! But naturally you do; of course you do.

[*Awkward pause.* MRS. SPARSIT *resumes her work, occasionally giving a small cough.*]

BOUNDERBY:
Should these events come to pass, and I am confident they shall, I imagine it would not be agreeable to a character like yours to remain here, though you would be very welcome here?

MRS. SPARSIT:
Oh dear no, sir, I could on no account think of that!

[MRS. SPARSIT *coughs again.*]

BOUNDERBY:
However, ma'am, there are apartments at my bank, where a born and bred lady, as keeper of the place, would be rather a catch than otherwise—

MRS. SPARSIT:
Sir, the proposal is like yourself, and if the position I should assume at the bank is one that I could occupy without descending lower in the social scale—

BOUNDERBY:
Why, of course it is.

MRS. SPARSIT:
Mr. Bounderby, you are very considerate.

BOUNDERBY:
You'll have your own private apartments, and you'll be what I take the liberty of considering precious comfortable.

MRS. SPARSIT:
I accept your offer gratefully. And I hope, sir, I fondly hope that Miss Gradgrind may be all you desire and deserve!


## FATHER AND DAUGHTER

[*Music/transition. A desk and two chairs indicate* MR. GRAD-GRIND's *study at Stone Lodge.*]

MR. GRADGRIND:
Louisa, my dear, you are the subject of a proposal of marriage.

[LOUISA *is silent.* MR. GRADGRIND *speaks.*]

A proposal of marriage, my dear.

LOUISA:
I hear you, Father. I am attending, I assure you.

MR. GRADGRIND:
Well! You are even more dispassionate than I expected, Louisa. Mr. Bounderby has informed me that he has long watched your progress and hoped that the time might arrive when he should offer you his hand in marriage. That time is now come.

[*Silence between them. A clock ticks loudly.*]

LOUISA:
Father, do you think I love Mr. Bounderby?

MR. GRADGRIND:
Well, my child, I—really—cannot take upon myself to say.

LOUISA:
Father, do you ask me to love Mr. Bounderby?

MR. GRADGRIND:
My dear Louisa, no. No. I ask nothing.

LOUISA:
Father, does Mr. Bounderby ask me to love him?

MR. GRADGRIND:
Really, my dear, it is difficult to answer your question—

LOUISA:
Difficult to answer it yes or no, Father?

MR. GRADGRIND:

Certainly, my dear. Because, because the reply depends on the sense in which we use the expression. Now Mr. Bounderby does not do you the injustice of pretending to anything fanciful, fantastic, or sentimental. Therefore, perhaps the expression itself may be a little misplaced.

LOUISA:

What would you advise me to use in its stead, Father?

MR. GRADGRIND:

Why, my dear Louisa, I would advise you to consider this question simply as one of tangible Fact. Now, what are the facts of this case? You are, we will say in round numbers, twenty years of age; Mr. Bounderby is, we will say in round numbers, fifty. There is some disparity in your respective years, but in your means and positions there is a great suitability—

LOUISA:

What do you recommend, Father, that I should substitute for the term I used just now? For the misplaced expression?

MR. GRADGRIND:

Confining yourself rigidly to Fact, the question of Fact you state to yourself is: Does Mr. Bounderby ask me to marry him? Yes, he does. The sole remaining question then is: Shall I marry him? I think nothing can be plainer than that.

LOUISA:

Shall I marry him?

MR. GRADGRIND:

Precisely. I now leave you to judge for yourself, my dear Louisa, it is for you to decide.

[*Music.* LOUISA *looks for a long time out the window at the town. Circus imagery shows what she is imagining, what she will never have, a scene between a man and a woman. The routine is romantic, filled with longing and passion; at times it looks as though the lovers are flying over the town.*]

Are you consulting the chimneys of the Coketown works, Louisa?

LOUISA:

There seems to be nothing there but languid and monotonous smoke. Yet when the night comes, fire bursts out, Father!

[LOUISA *shakes her head, and the vision disappears, but the music continues.*]

MR. GRADGRIND:

That is a fact, but I fail to see the application of that remark.

LOUISA:

Let it be so. Since Mr. Bounderby likes to take me thus, I am satisfied to accept his proposal. Tell him, Father, as soon as you please, that this was my answer. Repeat it, word for word, if you can, because I should wish him to know what I said.

MR. GRADGRIND:

It is quite right, my dear, to be exact. I will send off at once and let Mr. Bounderby know the good news. Have you any wish in reference to the period of your marriage, my child?

LOUISA:
None, Father. What does it matter?

[*The scene fades, and there is one more image of the entwined lovers in the air as* LOUISA *stares out the window.*]

# ACT TWO

## EFFECTS IN THE BANK

[MRS. SPARSIT *is in her new environs, having tea. The day is ending.* BITZER *reports to her.*]

MRS. SPARSIT:
The bank is shut up, Bitzer?

BITZER:
All is shut up, ma'am.

MRS. SPARSIT:
And what is the news of the day? Anything?

BITZER:
Well, ma'am, I can't say that I have heard anything particular. Our people are a bad lot, ma'am; but that is no news, unfortunately.

MRS. SPARSIT:

What are the restless wretches doing now?

BITZER:

Uniting, and leaguing, and engaging to stand by one another, ma'am. There are rumors of a strike impending in the mills.

MRS. SPARSIT:

It is much to be regretted that the united masters allow of any such unionizing among the lower classes.

BITZER:

Yes, ma'am.

MRS. SPARSIT:

Has it been a busy day, Bitzer?

BITZER:

Not a very busy day, my lady. About an average day.

MRS. SPARSIT:

The clerks are trustworthy, punctual, and industrious, of course?

BITZER:

Yes, ma'am, pretty fair, ma'am. With the usual exception.

MRS. SPARSIT:

Ah-h!

BITZER:

Mr. Thomas, ma'am, I doubt Mr. Thomas very much, ma'am; I don't like his ways at all.

MRS. SPARSIT:

Ah-h!

BITZER:

He is as improvident as any of the people in this town.

MRS. SPARSIT:

They would do well to take example by you, Bitzer.

BITZER:

Thank you, ma'am. I don't spend all of my wages, though they're not high, ma'am. Why can't they do as I have done, ma'am? What one person can do, another can do. As to their wanting recreations, ma'am, it's stuff and nonsense. I don't want recreations. I never did, and I never shall; I don't like 'em.

MRS. SPARSIT:

Waste of time and money!

BITZER:

I am sure we are constantly hearing, ma'am, till it becomes quite nauseous, concerning their wives and families. Why, look at me, ma'am! I don't want a wife and family. Why should they?

MRS. SPARSIT:

Because they are improvident.

BITZER:

Yes, ma'am, that's where it is. If they were more provident they would say, "I have only one to feed, and that's the person I most like to feed."

MRS. SPARSIT [*eating a muffin*]:
To be sure.

BITZER:
Thank you, ma'am. I shouldn't wish to disturb you at your tea, ma'am, but there's a gentleman outside and he has come across as if he was going to knock.

[*The gentleman appears and knocking is heard.*]

Would you wish the gentleman to be shown in, ma'am?

MRS. SPARSIT:
Yes, Bitzer.

[BITZER *goes to let the gentleman in.*]

What a stranger can want at the Bank at this time of evening I don't know, but I will see him.

[HARTHOUSE *enters.*]

Good evening, sir.

HARTHOUSE:
Mr. James Harthouse. I beg your pardon, pray excuse me. . . . I left my servant at the railway looking after the luggage and strolled on, looking about me. Exceedingly odd place. Will you allow me to ask you if it's always as black as this?

MRS. SPARSIT:
In general much blacker.

HARTHOUSE:

Is it possible! You are not a native, I think?


MRS. SPARSIT:

No, sir. It was once my good or ill fortune, as it may be—before I became a widow—to move in a very different sphere.


HARTHOUSE:

Hmmm. You must be very bored here?


MRS. SPARSIT:

I am the servant of circumstances, sir, and I have long adapted myself to the governing power of my life.


HARTHOUSE:

Very philosophical and very exemplary and laudable, and . . .


[HARTHOUSE *trails off wearily.*]


MRS. SPARSIT:

May I be permitted to ask, sir, to what I am indebted for the favor of—


HARTHOUSE:

Assuredly. Much obliged to you for reminding me. I am the bearer of a letter of introduction to Mr. Bounderby the banker. I presume that he does not reside in the edifice in which I have the honor of offering this explanation?


MRS. SPARSIT:

No sir, he does not.

HARTHOUSE:

Thank you. I thought I would just stroll on over to the bank to kill time, and having the good fortune to observe at the window a lady of a very superior and agreeable appearance, I considered that I could not do better than take the liberty of asking that lady where Mr. Bounderby the banker does live. Which I accordingly venture. My letter—here it is—is from the parliamentary representative from this place—Gradgrind—whom I have had the pleasure of knowing in London.

MRS. SPARSIT:

I don't need to see it, sir, and I'll get you the directions directly. May I ask what brings you to Coketown?

HARTHOUSE:

Certainly not vacationing . . . I have no idea, really, something governmental.

[She gives him the address.]

HARTHOUSE:

Thousand thanks. Of course, you know the banker well?

MRS. SPARSIT:

Yes, sir, in my dependent relation towards him, I have known him ten years.

HARTHOUSE:

Quite an eternity! I think he married Gradgrind's daughter?

MRS. SPARSIT:

Yes. He had that—honor.

HARTHOUSE:

The lady is quite a philosopher, I am told.


MRS. SPARSIT:

Indeed, sir, is she?


HARTHOUSE:

I see, by your meaning smile, you think not. As to age, now. Forty! Five-and-thirty?


MRS. SPARSIT:

A chit. Not twenty when she was married.


HARTHOUSE:

The father's manner prepared me for a grim and stony maturity. I am obliged to you for correcting so absurd a mistake. Pray excuse my intrusion. Many thanks. Good evening!


[HARTHOUSE *leaves, languishing down the street.*]


MRS. SPARSIT:

What do you think of the gentleman, Bitzer?


BITZER:

Spends a deal of money on his dress, ma'am.


MRS. SPARSIT:

It must be admitted that it's very tasteful.


BITZER:

Yes, ma'am, if that's worth the money. Besides which, ma'am, he looks to me as though he gamed.

MRS. SPARSIT:
It's immoral to game.

BITZER:
It's ridiculous.

MRS. SPARSIT:
Good evening, Bitzer.

BITZER:
Good evening, ma'am.

[*Music.* MRS. SPARSIT *looks out a window. As the scene shifts to the next location, what she sees in her mind's eye appears:* BOUNDERBY *shaking hands with* HARTHOUSE.]

MRS. SPARSIT:
Oh, you Noodle!


## MR. JAMES HARTHOUSE

[*At* BOUNDERBY'S.]

BOUNDERBY:
Well, Mr. James Harthouse, any friend of Gradgrind's is a friend of mine, but don't you deceive yourself by supposing for a moment that I am a gentleman as you clearly are. I am a bit of dirty riffraff and a genuine scrap of tag, rag, and bobtail!

HARTHOUSE:
Well, I find that very intriguing, sir.

BOUNDERBY:
And Coketown is not the kind of place you have been accustomed to.

HARTHOUSE:
But I am finding it quite charming, I assure you.

BOUNDERBY:
Well, don't be too sure of that. You see our smoke. That's meat and drink to us. It's the healthiest thing in the world in all respects and particularly for the lungs.

HARTHOUSE:
Yes, it's quite bracing.

BOUNDERBY:
I am glad to hear it. Now you have heard a lot of talk about our mills?

HARTHOUSE:
Mr. Gradgrind has talked glowingly about the mills.

BOUNDERBY:
Very good. It is the pleasantest work there is, and it's the lightest work there is, and it's the best paid work there is. We couldn't improve the mills unless we laid down Turkey carpets on the floor. Which we're not a-going to do.

HARTHOUSE:
Perfectly right, Mr. Bounderby.

BOUNDERBY:
As to our Hands, sir, their one object is to be fed on turtle soup and

venison with a gold spoon. They're complaining and plotting some nefarious action as we speak! But they're not a-going to get the gold spoon from me—none of 'em—ever. And now you know the place.

HARTHOUSE:
Sir, I am in the highest degree instructed by this condensed epitome of the whole Coketown question.

BOUNDERBY:
So now I'll introduce you to my wife. [*Calling to* LOUISA] Loo! Perhaps you know I married Tom Gradgrind's daughter?

HARTHOUSE:
Yes, Mr. Bounderby.

[LOUISA *enters.*]

BOUNDERBY:
Loo, Mr. James Harthouse. Mr. Harthouse has joined your father's ranks in Parliament. Mr. Harthouse, my wife Louisa. She has lots of expensive knowledge, sir, political and otherwise. If you want to cram for a test you won't find a better adviser than Loo Bounderby!

HARTHOUSE:
I could never be recommended to a more agreeable adviser. . . .

BOUNDERBY:
Come! If you're in the complimentary line, you'll get on here, for you'll meet with no competition. I despise the art of paying compliments. But your bringing up was different from mine; mine was a real thing, by George!

HARTHOUSE:

Mr. Bounderby is a noble animal in a comparatively natural state, quite free from the harness in which a conventional hack like myself works.

LOUISA:

You respect Mr. Bounderby very much. It is natural that you should.

[HARTHOUSE *coughs.*]

Mr. Bounderby tells me you are going to devote yourself to the service of your country and show the nation the way out of its difficulties.

HARTHOUSE:

Mrs. Bounderby, upon my honor, no. I will make no such pretense to you. I have seen a little, here and there, and have found it all to be quite worthless. I am going in for your respected father's opinions—really because I have no opinions and may as well back them as anything else.

LOUISA:

Have you none of your own?

HARTHOUSE:

God, no!

[TOM *arrives; cool* LOUISA's *face lights up with a big smile.* TOM *is sulky and sullen.* HARTHOUSE *notes this, very interested in* LOUISA's *sudden warmth.*]

LOUISA:

Tom!


BOUNDERBY:

When I was your age, young Tom, I didn't make my family wait on me. I was punctual!


TOM:

When you were my age you hadn't a wrong balance to get right and hadn't to dress afterwards.


BOUNDERBY:

Never mind that now.


TOM:

Well then, don't begin with me.


HARTHOUSE:

Mrs. Bounderby, your brother, I assume?


LOUISA:

Yes. Tom, love, here is Mr.—


HARTHOUSE:

Harthouse.


LOUISA:

He's a Parliament friend of Father's.


TOM:

Good evening, sir.

HARTHOUSE:
Good evening. Well, it has been a perfect delight to meet all of you, but I must take my leave.

BOUNDERBY:
Come back tomorrow, Mr. Harthouse, and I'll teach you more about this Coketown we call home. Thomas, you will escort Mr. Harthouse back to his hotel.

## THE WHELP

[*Music/transition. As the scene shifts, there are sounds of the street. The scene takes place as* HARTHOUSE *and* TOM *walk to* HARTHOUSE's *hotel, with* HARTHOUSE *offering* TOM *a cigar and drinks from a flask.*]

HARTHOUSE:
Do you smoke, young Mr. Gradgrind?

TOM:
Certainly.

HARTHOUSE [*holding out a flask*]:
Care for a tipple?

TOM:
Thank you. Now I suppose you'll pull out a deck of cards!

HARTHOUSE:
Ah, he games as well. . . .

TOM:
Of course, Mr. Harthouse!

HARTHOUSE:
We must play sometime. . . .

TOM:
That would be grand.

[*They walk in silence a moment.*]

Well, I hope you have had about a dose of old Bounderby tonight.

HARTHOUSE:
A very good fellow indeed!

TOM:
You think so? Oh, Lord . . .

HARTHOUSE:
You are a piece of caustic, Tom.

TOM:
Well, I've never cared for old Bounderby, and I am not going to begin to be polite now.

HARTHOUSE:
Don't mind me, but take care when his wife is by, you know.

TOM:
His wife? My sister, Loo? Oh yes! She never cared for old Bounderby!

HARTHOUSE:

That's the past tense, Tom. We are in the present tense, now.


TOM:

Third-person singular: she does not care!


HARTHOUSE:

Good! Very quaint! Though you don't mean it.


TOM:

Don't tell me you really suppose my sister Loo does care for old Bounderby?


HARTHOUSE:

My dear fellow, what am I bound to suppose when I find two married people living in harmony and happiness?


TOM:

You know our father, Mr. Harthouse, and therefore you needn't be surprised. She never had a lover, and the governor proposed old Bounderby, and she took him.


HARTHOUSE:

Very dutiful in your interesting sister.


TOM:

Yes, but she wouldn't have been as dutiful if it hadn't been for me. I persuaded her. I was stuck in Bounderby's bank and knew I'd have it easier if she married him. It was very game of her, wasn't it?


HARTHOUSE:

And she gets on so placidly.

TOM:

Oh, a girl can get on anywhere. She don't mind. Besides, Loo's not a common sort of girl. She can shut herself up within herself and think for an hour at a stretch.

HARTHOUSE:

Has resources of her own.

TOM:

Well, here you are. Yours is a very good tobacco, Mr. Harthouse, although be it a bit mild. Good night!

HARTHOUSE:

Good night.


## MEN AND BROTHERS

*[At the mill. Sounds of a rally.]*

SLACKBRIDGE:

Oh, my friends, the downtrodden operatives of Coketown! I tell you that the hour is come when we must rally round one another as one united power! We must honor our fathers who worked themselves to death for nothing in these mills! Honor our uncles and grandfathers who died mining in the pit of Old Hell's Shaft! And honor ourselves by rising up in anger against this history of oppression!

*[Shouts of "Hear, hear!" and "Hurrah!"]*

But oh, my friends and brothers! There is a man among us, a work-

ingman, who will not join us! Come forward and speak for yourself, Stephen Blackpool. . . .

[STEPHEN *steps forward.* RACHAEL *is there watching.*]

STEPHEN:
My friends, I'm the Hand as don't come in with the proposed reg-
ulations. I cannot come in with them. I have my reasons. . . . I made
a promise that I cannot break. My brothers, I know well all what's
afore me. I know you will have no more ado with a man who is not
with you in this matter. All I ask is that you let me work solitary
among you. I make no complaint of being outcasted, but I hope I
shall be let to work.

[STEPHEN *shuffles out. As he leaves,* BITZER, *who has been lurking
nearby, speaks quietly to him.* RACHAEL *watches from a distance.*]


## MEN AND MASTERS

[*Music.* BITZER *leads* STEPHEN *to* BOUNDERBY's *house and into a
room where* BOUNDERBY, HARTHOUSE, THOMAS, *and* LOUISA *are
gathered.*]

BOUNDERBY:
Well, Stephen, what's this I hear? What have these pests of the
earth been doing to you?

STEPHEN:
With your pardon, sir, I have nothing to say about it.

BOUNDERBY:
Now look here, Harthouse, here's a specimen of the Coketown

Hands. When he was last here, what was it, a year ago, Blackpool, I warned this man against the mischievous strangers who are always about! Now, although they have put this mark upon him, he is such a slave to them that he's afraid to open his lips about them!

STEPHEN:
I said as I had nothing to say, sir; not as I was fearful of opening my lips.

BOUNDERBY:
Oh, I know what you said! Now watch this, Harthouse, and see a tidy specimen of the Coketown problem! Mr. Blackpool, how does it happen that you refuse to be in this Combination?

STEPHEN:
I have passed a promise.

BOUNDERBY:
Not to me, you know.

STEPHEN:
Oh no, sir.

BOUNDERBY:
If only Josiah Bounderby of Coketown had been in question, you would have joined and made no bones about it?

STEPHEN:
Yes, sir.

BOUNDERBY:
Though he knows that these are a set of rascals and rebels!

STEPHEN [*addressing himself to* LOUISA]:
Nay, ma'am, not rebels and rascals. There's not a man among them
but believes he is doing his duty to the rest and to himself. Be sure
of that, ma'am.

BOUNDERBY:
If you will favor *me* with your attention for half a minute, here is
a Parliament gentleman from London. I should like him to hear a
short bit of dialogue between you and me. Now, what do you complain of?

STEPHEN:
I have not come here to complain. I come for that I were sent for.

BOUNDERBY:
What do you people, in a general way, complain of?

STEPHEN:
Well, we are in a muddle, sir. Look round town—so rich as it is—
and see the numbers of people brought into being here for to
weave and to piece out a living, all the same one way twixt their
cradles and their graves. Look how we live, and where we live, and
in what numbers; and look how the mills is always a-going and
how they never works us no closer to any distant object—except
death. Look how you writes of us and talks of us and how you are
always right and how we are always wrong. Who can look on it, sir,
and tell a man 'tis not a muddle?

BOUNDERBY:
I'll tell you something toward it, at any rate. We will make an example of half a dozen of these union leaders. We'll indict the black-
guards for felony and get 'em shipped off to penal settlements!

STEPHEN:

'Tis not with them the trouble begins, sir. This muddle were here before you and I were born and will go on long after we're dead! The strong hand will never fix it. Regulating them like they was figures in a sum or machines without loves and likings . . . this will never do it.

[LOUISA *watches and listens intently.*]

LOUISA [*quietly, to herself*]:
Figures in a sum . . .

BOUNDERBY:

Stop! I am on the gold spoon lookout! Now I see that you are one of those chaps who have always got a grievance . . . you go about sowing it and raising crops. You are such a bad chap that even your own union will have nothing to do with you. I never thought those fellows could be right in anything, but I'll tell you what, I'll have nothing to do with you either!

STEPHEN:
Sir, you know well that if I cannot get work with you, I cannot get it elsewhere.

BOUNDERBY:
I have no more to say about it.

STEPHEN:
Heaven help us all in this world.

# FADING AWAY

[*Coming out of* BOUNDERBY's, STEPHEN *sees* RACHAEL.]

RACHAEL:
Stephen!

STEPHEN:
Rachael, my dear!

RACHAEL:
I heard what you said at the meeting. Heaven bless thee, Stephen . . . and I saw that fellow bring you to the master's house. . . .

STEPHEN:
Not master anymore.

RACHAEL:
Have you left his work, Stephen?

STEPHEN:
Whether I have left his work or his work has left me it comes to the same. 'Tis as well so; it would have brought trouble if I had stayed.

RACHAEL:
Where will you go?

STEPHEN:
I don't know yet, Rachael.

[*The* OLD WOMAN *appears.*]

OLD WOMAN:
Young man . . .

STEPHEN:
Missus, you here?

OLD WOMAN:
It is my visiting time again, and I've been waiting to catch a glimpse of my gentleman and his new wife.

STEPHEN:
Well, missus, I have seen the lady and she were young and handsome. With fine dark thinking eyes and a still way.

OLD WOMAN:
Young and handsome. Yes! As bonny as a rose! And what a happy wife!

STEPHEN:
I suppose she be. . . .

OLD WOMAN:
Suppose she be? She must be. She's your master's wife.

STEPHEN:
Come to my poor place, missus, and take a cup of tea. If you come maybe Rachael will come, too. It may be long before I have the chance of thy company again, Rachael.

RACHAEL:
Yes, I'll come.

[*As they begin to walk through the streets and the following scene begins,* LOUISA *comes out of* BOUNDERBY'S *with* TOM *and follows at a distance.*]

STEPHEN:
I have never thought yet, missus, of asking thy name.

OLD WOMAN:
Mrs. Pegler.

STEPHEN:
Widow, I think?

MRS. PEGLER:
Oh, many long years!

STEPHEN:
Any children?

MRS. PEGLER [*rattled*]:
No, not now, not now.

STEPHEN:
Oh, I'm sorry. . . .

MRS. PEGLER:
I had a son and he did well, wonderfully well. But he is not to be spoken of, if you please. He is—I have lost him.

STEPHEN:
I'm sorry I have spoken on it. . . .

[STEPHEN, RACHAEL, *and* MRS. PEGLER *arrive at* STEPHEN's *house. There is a knock at the door. It is* LOUISA *and* TOM.]

Mrs. Bounderby!

[MRS. PEGLER *runs to a corner to hide herself.* LOUISA *and* TOM *enter.*]

LOUISA:
I have come to speak to you in consequence of what passed just now. Is this your wife?

[*Awkward pause.*]

I remember, I recollect, I have heard your domestic misfortunes spoken of. I did not mean to pain anyone here. . . . [*To* RACHAEL] He has told you what has passed between himself and my husband?

RACHAEL:
I have heard the end of it, young lady.

LOUISA:
Being rejected by one employer, he will probably be rejected by all?

RACHAEL:
The chances are next to nothing for a man who gets a bad name among them.

LOUISA:
What will you do?

STEPHEN:
Well, ma'am, I must quit this part and try another.

LOUISA:
How will you travel?


STEPHEN:
Afoot, my kind lady, afoot.


[LOUISA *pulls out some money.*]


LOUISA [*to* RACHAEL]:
Will you tell him—for you know how, without offense—that this is freely his, to help him on his way?


RACHAEL:
Bless you for thinking of the poor man with such tenderness. But 'tis for him to know his heart and what is right according to it.


STEPHEN:
You don't need Rachael to make your offer any kinder, young lady. I'll borrow some of it for to pay it back.


[LOUISA *gives* STEPHEN *money; he returns most of it.*]


Thank you, young lady. . . .


TOM:
Just wait a moment, Loo! I should like to speak to him a moment. Something comes into my head. If you'll step out on the stairs, Blackpool, I'll mention it.


[TOM *and* STEPHEN *step out; the focus shifts to them.*]


I say! I think I can do you a good turn. I can't tell you what it is, because it may not come to anything. But there's no harm in my trying. When are you off?

STEPHEN:
Friday or Saturday, nigh about.

TOM:
Very well. When you leave work on the days before your going away, just hang about the bank an hour or so, will you? I work there, you know, and if I find I can do you the service I want to I'll have someone bring a note or message to you outside where you are waiting. You are sure you understand?

STEPHEN:
I understand, sir.

TOM:
Don't make any mistake, then, and don't forget. I shall tell my sister as we go home what I have in view, and she'll approve. All right?

[TOM *looks in the door.*]

Come along, Loo!

[TOM *and* LOUISA *exit.*]

MRS. PEGLER:
Oh, I should be leaving, too. Oh, what a pretty dear she was . . . so lovely. Thank you so much for your hospitality. I'm sorry for your troubles.

[MRS. PEGLER *leaves.*]

STEPHEN:
I shall strive to see thee again, Rachael, before I go, but if not—

RACHAEL:
Thou wilt not, Stephen, I know. 'Tis better that we be open with one another.

STEPHEN:
Thou art always right, Rachael.

RACHAEL:
Thou will write to me, and tell me all that happens?

STEPHEN:
Yes. Heaven bless thee, Rachael.

RACHAEL:
May it bless thee, Stephen, too, in all thy wanderings and send thee peace and rest at last!

STEPHEN:
Good night. Good-bye!

[*Music/transitional sequence of time passing.* STEPHEN *hangs around the bank;* BITZER *and* MRS. SPARSIT *notice him, then* STEPHEN *heads out of town.*]


GUNPOWDER

[*The focus shifts to* LOUISA *sitting on a bench outside on the grounds of* BOUNDERBY's *house, in contemplation.* HARTHOUSE *approaches her.*]

HARTHOUSE:

Mrs. Bounderby, I esteem it a most fortunate accident that I find you alone here. I have for some time had a particular wish to speak to you. Your brother, my young friend Tom—

LOUISA [*her face lighting up*]:
Yes?

HARTHOUSE:

Pardon me, but the expression of your sisterly interest is so beautiful—I know this is inexcusable, but I am so compelled to admire—

LOUISA:
I am waiting for your further reference to my brother.

HARTHOUSE:

You are rigid with me, and I deserve it. I have an interest in your brother.

LOUISA:
Have you an interest in anything, Mr. Harthouse?

HARTHOUSE:

If you had asked me when I first came here, I should have said no. I must say now—even at the hazard of appearing to make a pretense—yes.

LOUISA:
Well, I will give you credit for being interested in my brother.

HARTHOUSE:

Thank you. Mrs. Bounderby, it is no irrevocable offense in a young fellow of your brother's years if he is inconsiderate and expensive. I certainly was. Allow me to be frank. Do you think he games at all?

LOUISA:

I think he makes bets. I know he does.

HARTHOUSE:

May I hint at the probability of your sometimes supplying him with money?

[LOUISA *doesn't answer.*]

I ask for his sake, my dear Mrs. Bounderby. I think Tom may be falling into trouble, and as one who has been in trouble himself, I want to stretch out a helping hand.

[LOUISA *doesn't answer.*]

[*Indicating the bench*] May I?

[LOUISA *nods and makes room for him.*]

Mrs. Bounderby, may there be a better confidence between yourself and me? Tom has borrowed a considerable sum of you?

LOUISA:

I have sold what were just trinkets to me in the past, to help him. Lately he has asked me for a sum of one hundred pounds. I have not been able to give it to him and I feel uneasy. . . . I have told no one else. . . .

HARTHOUSE:

Mrs. Bounderby, I perceive that Tom really has no man to help redirect him. I would like to be that man, for I see much of myself in Tom. I have one great fault to find with him, however, which I cannot forgive.

LOUISA:

What fault is that?

HARTHOUSE:

I cannot forgive him for not being more sensible of the affection of his best friend; of the devotion of his best friend; of her unselfishness; of her sacrifice. The return he makes her, from my observations, is a very poor one.

[*Pause.* LOUISA *is moved.*]

Oh, God, I seem to be protesting that I am a sort of good fellow, when upon my honor . . .

[HARTHOUSE *catches sight of* TOM *entering.*]

I see your brother coming now. Tom!

TOM:

Oh! I didn't know you were here.

HARTHOUSE:

Whose name, Tom, have you been carving on the trees?

TOM:

Whose name? Oh! You mean what girl's name?

HARTHOUSE:

You have a suspicious appearance of inscribing some fair creature's on the bark, Tom.

TOM:

Not much of that, Mr. Harthouse, unless some fair creature with a slashing fortune at her own disposal would take a fancy to me.

HARTHOUSE:

I'm afraid you are mercenary, Tom.

TOM:

Who is not mercenary? Ask my sister.

LOUISA:

Have you so proved it to be a failing of mine, Tom?

TOM:

You know whether the cap fits you, Loo. If it does, you can wear it.

HARTHOUSE:

Tom is misanthropical today, as all bored people are now and then. Don't believe him, Mrs. Bounderby. Tom, I want to have a word with you alone.

[HARTHOUSE *nods to* LOUISA, *who leaves them, moving away and watching from a distance.*]

Tom, what's the matter?

TOM:

Oh! Mr. Harthouse, you have no idea what a state I have got myself into—what a state my sister could get me out of, if she would only have done it.

HARTHOUSE:

Tom, you expect too much of your sister. You have had money of her before and if she has not got it now—

TOM:

But she could get it. Why didn't she get it out of old Bounderby for my sake? She doesn't have to say why. But no. There she sits in his company like a stone and me facing real trouble!

HARTHOUSE:

What is the present need, Tom? Three figures? Say what they are. Let me be your banker!

TOM:

For God's sake, don't talk of bankers! Mr. Harthouse, it's too late. I needed it before, if it was to be of use to me. But thank you, you're a true friend.

[TOM *shakes* HARTHOUSE's *hand, then throws himself at him in a hug.*]

HARTHOUSE:

Tom, I am desperately intent on your softening towards your sister and on your being a more loving and agreeable sort of brother.

TOM:

I will be, Mr. Harthouse.

HARTHOUSE:

No time like the present, Tom. Begin at once.

TOM:
Loo!

[LOUISA *crosses to* TOM.]

I didn't mean to be cross, Loo. I know you are fond of me, and you know I am fond of you.

[TOM *and* LOUISA *embrace.* LOUISA *smiles, beaming toward* HARTHOUSE.]

HARTHOUSE:
Well, my friends, we will tear ourselves asunder until tomorrow. . . .

[*Music/transition. As night falls,* TOM *takes* LOUISA's *arm and leads her into the house.* HARTHOUSE *follows with his eyes and exits. After* TOM *deposits* LOUISA *inside, he looks around to make sure he is alone and races off into the night.*]


EXPLOSION

[*The next evening.* HARTHOUSE *is on his way to* BOUNDERBY's *when* BOUNDERBY *comes running toward the house.* LOUISA, MRS. SPARSIT, *and* BITZER *follow.*]

BOUNDERBY:
Harthouse, have you heard? The bank's robbed!

HARTHOUSE:
You don't mean it!

BOUNDERBY:
Last night. With a false key.

HARTHOUSE:
Of how much?

BOUNDERBY:
Not more than a hundred and fifty pound. But it's not the sum; it's the fact. Young Tom locked a hundred and fifty odd pound in his safe at the bank—

BITZER:
One hundred fifty-four and seventy-one pence.

BOUNDERBY:
Do not interrupt! It's enough to be robbed while you're snoring nearby without being corrected with your seventy-one pence! Young Tom locked up the money, and sometime in the night, while this fellow snored, some fellows abstracted the contents. Their false key was found in the street.

BITZER [*producing the key*]:
False key, sir!

[BOUNDERBY *glares at* BITZER.]

HARTHOUSE:
Where is Tom?

BOUNDERBY:
He has been helping the police all day.

HARTHOUSE:

Is anyone suspected?


BOUNDERBY:

Josiah Bounderby of Coketown is not to be plundered and nobody suspected! What should you say to . . . to a Hand being in it?


HARTHOUSE:

Not our friend Blackpot?


BOUNDERBY:

Blackpool, that's the man.


LOUISA:

No!


BOUNDERBY:

Oh yes! I know, they are the finest people in the world, these fellows. They have the gift of gab. They only want to have their rights explained to them. But what do you say to his being seen watching the bank? To Mrs. Sparsit and Bitzer seeing him and thinking he could be lurking for no good!


HARTHOUSE:

Suspicious, certainly.


BOUNDERBY:

I think so. But there are more of them in it. There's an old woman. She watches the place a whole day before this fellow begins! Bitzer, go to the bank and send young Tom home if you think you can handle the task! And such bloody bad timing with my upcoming business in Canterbury!

[BITZER *leaves.* BOUNDERBY *takes* MRS. SPARSIT's *arm.*]

Loo, here's Mrs. Sparsit to look after. Her nerves have been acted upon by this business, and she'll stay here with us for a week or so.

[BOUNDERBY *and* MRS. SPARSIT *begin to walk back to the house.* LOUISA *and* HARTHOUSE *stay outside, also linking arms.*]

MRS. SPARSIT:
Thank you, sir, but pray do not let my comfort be a consideration. Anything will do for me.

BOUNDERBY:
A woman of your upbringing needs comfort in times like these. You shall have your old room and will dine with us tomorrow!

MRS. SPARSIT:
Indeed, sir, you are very good. But I will dine in the kitchen on the simple mutton. . . .

BOUNDERBY:
Absolutely not, madam!

[MRS. SPARSIT *and* BOUNDERBY *have entered the house.* LOUISA *and* HARTHOUSE *are out on the grounds walking and conversing in the distance.*]

MRS. SPARSIT:
Don't be low, sir. Pray let me see you cheerful, sir, as I used to do.

BOUNDERBY:
It's hard to be cheerful when you've been plundered.

MRS. SPARSIT:

But, sir, I've noted this change in your disposition long before today, and I cannot bear to see you so. Try a hand at backgammon, sir, as you used to do when I had the honor of living under your roof.

BOUNDERBY:

I haven't played backgammon, ma'am, since that time.

MRS. SPARSIT:

No, sir. I am aware that you have not. I remember that Miss Gradgr—I mean Mrs. Bounderby—takes no interest in the game. But I shall be happy, sir, if you will condescend.

[*They sit near a window and play.* MRS. SPARSIT *looks out the window trying to see* HARTHOUSE *and* LOUISA.]

BOUNDERBY:

What's the matter, ma'am? You don't see a Fire, do you?

MRS. SPARSIT:

Oh dear no, sir. I was thinking of the dew.

BOUNDERBY:

What do you have to do with the dew, ma'am?

MRS. SPARSIT:

It's not myself, sir. I am fearful of Miss Gradgr—Mrs. Bounderby's taking cold.

BOUNDERBY:

She never takes cold.

MRS. SPARSIT:
Really, sir?

[*She coughs.*]

BOUNDERBY:
I'm too low to finish the game, ma'am. I will retire now.

MRS. SPARSIT:
Oh, sir? Not your sherry warm with lemon peel and nutmeg?

BOUNDERBY:
Why, I have got out of the habit of taking it now, ma'am.

MRS. SPARSIT:
The more's the pity, sir, you are losing all your good old habits.
Cheer up, sir. If Miss Gradgrind will permit me, I will offer to make
it for you, as I have often done. I will set it outside your door as in
the old days.

[BOUNDERBY *retires to his room.* MRS. SPARSIT *looks out the window, watching* HARTHOUSE *and* LOUISA *in the distance.* LOUISA *has her hand on* HARTHOUSE's *arm.*]

MRS. SPARSIT:
Ah, Miss Gradgrind—I have erected in my mind a mighty staircase
with a dark pit of shame and ruin at the bottom. Down those stairs
I see you coming. . . .

[*She looks again, as* HARTHOUSE *bows good-bye to* LOUISA.]

Your foot on another step of my staircase, lady, and all your art
shall never blind me.

[MRS. SPARSIT *lurks.* LOUISA *comes inside.* MRS. SPARSIT *and* LOUISA *pass each other.*]

LOUISA:
Has Tom come home yet?

MRS. SPARSIT:
No, Miss Gradgr—Mrs. Bounderby—although it is very late to still be out. . . .

[MRS. SPARSIT *goes off.* TOM *sneaks in. He's been followed by* BITZER, *who watches as* TOM *enters the house.* LOUISA *catches* TOM *as he comes inside.*]

LOUISA:
Tom . . . Tom, have you anything to tell me? If ever you have loved me in your life and have concealed anything from everyone, tell it to me.

TOM:
I don't know what you mean, Loo. You have been dreaming.

LOUISA:
You can tell me nothing that will change me. Oh, Tom, tell me the truth!

TOM:
I don't know what you mean, Loo!

LOUISA:
As you are here alone in the melancholy night, so you will be one night when even I shall have left you. In the name of that time, Tom, tell me the truth now!

TOM:

What is it you want to know?

LOUISA:

I will not reproach you. I will be compassionate and true to you. I will save you at whatever cost. Whisper very softly. Say only yes and I shall understand you!

[*She turns her ear toward him. He looks as though he's going to speak but then turns his head.*]

Not a word, Tom?

TOM:

How can I say yes, or how can I say no, when I don't know what you mean? Loo, I am so tired that I am sure I wonder I don't say anything to get to sleep. Go to bed.

[TOM *kisses* LOUISA; *she leaves. After she has gone,* TOM *sits on the stairs with his head in his hands, crying.*]

## LOWER AND LOWER

[*Music/transitional sequence: night passes; the next day dawns.* BOUNDERBY, *carrying a suitcase, bows good-bye to* MRS. SPARSIT. *As he goes out the door,* LOUISA *sees him leave from her window and grabs her hat and goes out.* MRS. SPARSIT *spies* LOUISA *leaving and grabs her coat to follow. Outside,* HARTHOUSE *grabs* LOUISA; *they have a heated conversation.* LOUISA *breaks away and goes to sit on a garden bench.* MRS. SPARSIT *lurks around, spying on them.*]

LOUISA:
Please, go away. I command you to go away.

[LOUISA *stays there, immobile; he puts his arm around her.*]

HARTHOUSE:
But Louisa . . .

LOUISA:
Not here.

HARTHOUSE:
Where, Louisa?

LOUISA:
Not here.

HARTHOUSE:
But my dearest Louisa, what could I do? Knowing you were alone, was it possible that I could stay away?

LOUISA:
Not here.

HARTHOUSE:
But we have so little time to make so much of, and I have come so far and am altogether so devoted and distracted. Louisa!

LOUISA:
Am I to say again that I must be left to myself here?

[*Thunder. Rain begins.* HARTHOUSE *takes off his jacket and puts it around* LOUISA's *shoulders.*]

HARTHOUSE:
But I'm the man who has seen how cast away you are. I am the
man that adores you! I must see you. . . .

LOUISA:
I'll meet you someplace else.

HARTHOUSE:
Where, my Louisa, where?

[LOUISA *whispers in* HARTHOUSE'*s ear.*]

MRS. SPARSIT:
Ha! She has fallen from the lowest stair and is swallowed up in the
gulf!

[LOUISA *and* HARTHOUSE *part as the storm begins to rage.* MRS.
SPARSIT *follows* LOUISA *as she runs through the streets of the
town. There is a confusion of women, and* MRS. SPARSIT *realizes
she has been following the wrong person.*]

I have lost her! I must fetch Mr. Bounderby from Canterbury!


DOWN

[LOUISA, *drenched from the rain and holding* HARTHOUSE'*s coat
over her head, enters* MR. GRADGRIND'*s study at Stone Lodge.* SISSY
*passes by the room, stops in the open doorway, and listens with
concern.*]

MR. GRADGRIND [*taking the wet coat and throwing it on his desk*]:
Louisa!

LOUISA:
Father, I want to speak to you.

MR. GRADGRIND:
What is the matter? Have you come here exposed to this storm?

LOUISA:
Father, you have trained me from my cradle. I curse the hour in which I was born to such a destiny—

MR. GRADGRIND:
Curse the hour?

LOUISA:
How could you give me life and take from me all the things that make life worth living? What have you done, oh, Father, with the garden that should have bloomed once in this great wilderness here! [*She strikes herself in the breast.*] I don't reproach you, Father. What you have never nurtured in me, you have never nurtured in yourself, but oh! if you only had what a better and happier creature I should be! Now, hear what I have come to say. Father, with an ardent impulse towards some region where rules were not absolute, I have grown up, battling every inch of my way. In this condition, Father, you proposed a husband to me. I took him. I never made a reference to him or you that I loved him. I was not wholly indifferent, for I had a hope of being pleasant and useful to my dear Tom. When I was irrevocably married, chance threw into my way a new acquaintance, a man such as I had had no experience of: used to the world, light, polished, easy, conveying to me that he understood me and read my thoughts. There seemed to be a near affinity between us. I only wondered why he who cared for nothing else would care for me—

MR. GRADGRIND:

For you, Louisa!


LOUISA:

I have not disgraced you. But if you ask me whether I have loved him, or do love him, it may be so. I don't know! This night, my husband being away, he has been with me, declaring himself my lover. This minute he expects me, for I could release myself of his presence by no other means. I do not know that I am sorry; I do not know that I am ashamed. All that I know is your philosophy and your teaching will not save me now. Father, you have brought me to this. Save me by some other means!

[LOUISA *falls to the floor.* SISSY *enters the room and helps* MR. GRADGRIND *get* LOUISA *up and off to her room.* SISSY *then picks up* HARTHOUSE's *coat and heads out the door.*]


## VERY RIDICULOUS

[HARTHOUSE *paces nervously in his room.*]

HARTHOUSE:

I am so incredibly bored! So, whether I am waiting for a hostile message, or one with further instructions, or an impromptu wrestle with my friend Bounderby, I may as well read the paper.

[*He struggles with the paper, tries to read.*]

Bounderby does have the advantage in point of weight, maybe I should go into training and then have a nice steak. . . .

[HARTHOUSE *tries to read again. There is a knock on the door. It is* SISSY.]

SISSY:
I speak to Mr. Harthouse?

HARTHOUSE:
To Mr. Harthouse. Please come in.

SISSY:
If I do not understand what your honor as a gentleman binds you to in other matters, I am sure I may rely upon it to keep my visit secret?

HARTHOUSE:
You may, I assure you.

SISSY:
You have already guessed whom I left just now?

HARTHOUSE:
I have been in the greatest concern during the last four-and-twenty hours on a lady's account. I hope you come from that lady?

SISSY:
I left her within an hour.

HARTHOUSE:
At—?

SISSY:
Her father's. You may be sure, sir, you will never see her again as long as you live.

[HARTHOUSE *draws a long breath.*]

HARTHOUSE:

So startling an announcement, so confidently made and by such lips, is really disconcerting. With no disrespect for your judgment and sincerity, excuse my saying that I cling to the belief that there is yet hope.

SISSY:

There is no more hope of your ever speaking with her again than there would be if she had died when she came home last night.

HARTHOUSE:

But if I can't believe that, or . . . or if I should by infirmity of nature be obstinate . . . may I ask if you've been charged to convey that information to me by the lady of whom we speak?

SISSY:

I have no charge of her. . . . I have only the commission of my love for her and her love for me. I have no further trust than that I know something of her character and her marriage. Oh, Mr. Harthouse, I think you had that trust, too!

HARTHOUSE:

Look, I am not a moral sort of fellow and I've never pretended to be one. At the same time I beg to assure you that I have had no particularly evil intentions but have glided on from one step to another with a smoothness so diabolical that I had not the slightest idea the catalog of my indiscretions was half so long until I begin to turn it over. Whereas I find that it is really in several volumes.

SISSY:

You must leave here immediately. I do not say that it is much compensation, or that it is enough; but it is something and it is necessary.

HARTHOUSE:
But do you know the extent of what you ask? You probably are not aware that I am here on a public kind of business which I am supposed to be devoted to in quite a desperate manner? You are probably not aware, but I assure you it's the fact.

[*No response from* SISSY.]

Besides which, it's so alarmingly absurd. It would make a man so ridiculous to back out of his work in such an incomprehensible way.

SISSY:
I am quite sure that it is the only reparation in your power, sir.

[HARTHOUSE *paces.*]

HARTHOUSE:
I don't know what to say. So immensely absurd!

[*More pacing.*]

If I were to do such a very ridiculous thing it could only be in the most inviolable confidence.

SISSY:
I will trust to you, and you will trust to me.

HARTHOUSE:

I see no way out of it. What will be, will be. I must take off myself,
I imagine—

SISSY:

Thank you, sir.

HARTHOUSE:

I must not only regard myself as being in a very ridiculous position but as being vanquished at all points.

[SISSY *starts to leave.*]

What is my enemy's name?

SISSY:

My name?

HARTHOUSE:

The only name I could possibly care to know tonight.

SISSY:

Sissy Jupe.

HARTHOUSE:

Related to the family?

SISSY:

I was separated from my father—he was a clown in the circus—
and taken pity on by Mr. Gradgrind. Good-bye, sir.

[SISSY *leaves.*]

HARTHOUSE:
It wanted this to complete the defeat. Only a poor circus girl—only James Harthouse a Great Pyramid of failure.

[*Pause.*]

Hmmm. The Pyramids . . .

[*He writes a note.*]

Dear Uncle Jack—All up at Coketown. Bored out of the place and going in for camels.


## VERY DECIDED

[*Music.* SISSY *returns to Stone Lodge. As soon as she enters, there is a knock at the door.*]

BOUNDERBY [*calling from outside*]:
Tom Gradgrind!

[SISSY *lets in* BOUNDERBY *and* MRS. SPARSIT.]

Now, Tom Gradgrind, here's a lady here who has something to say to you that will strike you dumb.

[MRS. SPARSIT *is coughing and sneezing; she has caught a terrible cold and can't speak.*]

If you can't get it out, ma'am, I will. Tom Gradgrind, Mrs. Sparsit found herself, by accident, in a situation to overhear a conversation between your daughter and your precious gentleman-friend Mr. James Harthouse. And in that conversation—

MR. GRADGRIND:
It is not necessary to repeat its tenor. I know what passed.

BOUNDERBY:
You do? Perhaps you know where your daughter is at the present time?

MR. GRADGRIND:
She is here.

BOUNDERBY:
Here?

MR. GRADGRIND:
The moment she could detach herself from that interview, Louisa hurried here, for protection.

[BOUNDERBY *turns on* MRS. SPARSIT.]

BOUNDERBY:
Now, ma'am! We shall be happy to hear any little apology you may think proper to offer, for going about the country at express pace, with no other luggage than a Cock-and-a-Bull!

MRS. SPARSIT:
Sir, my nerves are too much shaken and my health is too much impaired, in your service, to do anything more than take my refuge in tears.

[*Which she does.*]

BOUNDERBY:

Well, ma'am, you may take refuge in something else: a coach. Please take yourself home to the bank.

[MRS. SPARSIT *exits.*]

MR. GRADGRIND:

Bounderby, I see reason to doubt whether we have ever quite understood Louisa.

BOUNDERBY:

Who do you mean by "we"?

MR. GRADGRIND:

Let me say "I," then. I think there are qualities in Louisa which . . . which have been harshly neglected, and . . . and a little perverted. And . . . and I would suggest to you that . . . that if you would kindly leave her to her better nature for a while . . . it . . . it would be the better for the happiness of all of us.

[BOUNDERBY *turns crimson.*]

BOUNDERBY:

You'd like to keep her here for a time?

MR. GRADGRIND:

I . . . I had intended to recommend, my dear Bounderby, that you should allow Louisa to remain here on a visit and be attended by Sissy, who understands her and in whom she trusts.

BOUNDERBY:

Now, look you here, Tom Gradgrind. I am Josiah Bounderby of

Coketown. I know the bricks of this town, I know the smoke of this town, and I know the Hands of this town. I know 'em all pretty well. They're real. When a man tells me anything about imaginative qualities, I know what he means. He means turtle soup and venison with a gold spoon. That's what your daughter wants. She will never have it from me.

MR. GRADGRIND:
I hoped you would have taken a different tone.

BOUNDERBY:
You may not believe it, sir, but there are ladies—born ladies—belonging to families—Families!—who next to worship the ground I walk on. Highly connected females have been astonished to see the way your daughter has conducted herself. They have wondered how I have suffered it!

MR. GRADGRIND:
The less we say tonight the better, I think.

BOUNDERBY:
The more we say tonight, the better, I think. I am sending Louisa's things over, and you'll take charge of her for the future.

MR. GRADGRIND:
Let me seriously entreat you to reconsider this before you commit yourself to such a decision.

BOUNDERBY:
Whatever I do, I do at once. I have got no more to say. Good night!

# LOST AND FOUND

[*Before* BOUNDERBY *can leave, there is a commotion in the entranceway.* RACHAEL *enters, followed by* TOM.]

RACHAEL:
Mr. Bounderby—

TOM:
I'm sorry to barge in, Mr. Bounderby, Father, but this woman here practically accosted me at the bank and insisted I bring her to you. I refused, but she set out anyway.

RACHAEL:
Mr. Bounderby, I'm here to tell you that—

TOM:
I warn you, she's making no sense—

RACHAEL:
Yes, I am, young man, you was there and your sister, and I want you to tell the master—

BOUNDERBY:
Tell me what?

RACHAEL:
That they came to Stephen's house, my Stephen, who you've accused of robbing you!

BOUNDERBY:
Blackpool?

RACHAEL:
Yes—

[LOUISA *enters*.]

MR. GRADGRIND:
Louisa . . .

RACHAEL:
Young lady, you have seen me once before, young lady.

[TOM *coughs.*]

You have seen me, young lady. . . .

[TOM *coughs again.*]

LOUISA:
I have.

MR GRADGRIND:
What?

RACHAEL:
Will you make it known, young lady, where, and who was there?

LOUISA:
I went to the house where Stephen Blackpool lodged on the night
of his discharge from his work, and I saw you there. He was there,
too, and an old woman who did not speak. My brother was with me.

MR. GRADGRIND:
Why didn't you say so, Tom?

TOM:

I promised my sister I wouldn't. And besides, she tells her own story so precious well—and so full—that what business had I to take it out of her mouth!

RACHAEL:

Say, if you please, why you ever came to Stephen's that night.

LOUISA:

I felt compassion for him and wished to offer him assistance.

BOUNDERBY:

Thank you, ma'am. Much flattered and obliged.

RACHAEL:

Did you offer him money?

LOUISA:

Yes, but he refused most of it.

RACHAEL:

Young lady, Stephen Blackpool is now named as a thief in public print all over this town!

LOUISA:

I am very, very sorry.

RACHAEL:

I hope you may be, but I don't know! I can't tell but what you may have come that night with some aim of your own, not minding to what trouble you brought the poor man.

TOM:

You're a pretty article to come here with these precious imputations! You ought to be bundled out for not knowing how to behave yourself!

MR. GRADGRIND:

Tom!

LOUISA:

I pity him from my heart and I hope that he will clear himself.

RACHAEL:

You need have no fear of that, young lady, he is sure. I have written to him and he will be here today to clear his name!

[MRS. SPARSIT *bursts into the room, dragging a struggling woman with her. It is* MRS. PEGLER.]

MRS. SPARSIT:

Sir, it is my good fortune to produce a person you have much desired to find. When I arrived at the bank a few minutes ago, who should I see but the old woman involved in the robbery!

[MRS. PEGLER *is revealed to* BOUNDERBY, *who turns all possible colors.*]

RACHAEL:

Mrs. Pegler!

BOUNDERBY:

Why, what do you mean by this?

MRS. SPARSIT:
Sir!

BOUNDERBY:
How dare you go and poke your officious nose into my family affairs?

MRS. PEGLER:
My dear Josiah—

MRS. SPARSIT:
Your family affairs . . . ?

MRS. PEGLER:
It's not my fault, Josiah. I have always lived quiet and secret. I have never broken the condition once. I have never said I was your mother. I have admired you at a distance; and if I have come to town sometimes to take a proud peep at you, I have done it unbeknown, my love, and gone away again.

MR. GRADGRIND:
I am surprised, madam, that you have the face to claim Mr. Bounderby for your son, after your unnatural and inhuman treatment of him.

MRS. PEGLER:
God forgive you, sir. . . .

MR. GRADGRIND:
Do you deny, then, that you left your son to—to be brought up in the gutter?

MRS. PEGLER:

My dear boy knows and will tell you that he comes of parents that loved him as dear as the best could, and I'll give you to know, sir, he never forgot his old mother but pensioned me, only making the condition that I was to keep down in my own part and not trouble him. And it's right that I should keep down in my own part, and I have no doubts that if I was here I should do many unbefitting things, and I am well contented, and I can love for love's own sake!

MR. GRADGRIND:

But I don't understand—

BOUNDERBY:

I'm not bound to deliver a lecture on my family affairs, Tom Gradgrind! In reference to the bank robbery, there has been a mistake made concerning my mother. If there hadn't been overofficiousness, it wouldn't have been made! Good evening!

[As BOUNDERBY *is about to leave,* BITZER *runs into the room.*]

BITZER:

We've found Blackpool! He's fallen down Old Hell's Shaft!

RACHAEL:

Is he alive?

BITZER:

Yes, but he's hurt very bad. He said he was on his way to Mr. Bounderby's when he fell. He was coming back because he was innocent of what was laid to his charge. . . .

RACHAEL:

Oh, Stephen, Stephen!

# THE STARLIGHT

[*Music.* RACHAEL *runs out, and everyone follows. As they run, there is an image of* STEPHEN *falling a long distance. When they arrive at Old Hell's Shaft,* STEPHEN *is carried to* RACHAEL, *who cradles him on her lap. It is night, and they are away from the city for the first time, with stars instead of smoke above them.*]

RACHAEL:
Stephen!

STEPHEN:
Rachael. Rachael, my dear.

[*She takes his hand.*]

Don't let go.

RACHAEL:
Thou art in great pain, my own dear Stephen?

STEPHEN:
Not now. Ah, Rachael, what a muddle! I have fell into the pit, my dear, that has cost many men's lives. See how we workingmen die and no need one way or another! A muddle! If all things that touches us, my dear, was not so muddled, I shouldn't have had to come here. But look up yonder, Rachael! Look above!

[*She looks up at the stars.*]

That star has shined upon me in my pain and trouble down below. I have looked at it and thought of thee, Rachael, till the muddle in my mind have cleared away. When I got thy letter, I easily believed that there were a wicked plot between the young lady and her brother. When I fell, I were in anger with her. But looking up yonder—with it shining on me—I have seen more clear and have made it my dying prayer that all the world may only come together more and get a better understanding of one another than when I were in it my own weak self.

[LOUISA *bends down to him.*]

You have heard? I have not forgot you, lady.

LOUISA:
Yes, Stephen, I have heard you. And your prayer is mine.

STEPHEN:
You have a father. Will you take a message to him?

LOUISA:
He is here. Father . . .

[LOUISA *gets her father; he kneels down by* STEPHEN. SISSY *goes to* TOM *and speaks quietly. He slips away.*]

STEPHEN:
Sir, you will clear me and make my name good with all men. This I leave to you.

MR. GRADGRIND:
But how, my good man?

STEPHEN:
Sir, your son will tell you how. Ask him. I make no charges. I have

seen and spoken with your son, one night. I ask that you clear me—and I trust to you to do it. [*To* RACHAEL] Rachael, beloved lass! Don't let go my hand. We may walk together tonight, my dear! This is the night when we can walk together for all to see. . . .

RACHAEL:
I will hold thy hand and keep beside thee, Stephen, all the way.

STEPHEN:
Bless thee!

[STEPHEN *dies. He is lifted up and carried off in a funeral procession. As the others follow the procession,* MR. GRADGRIND, LOUISA, *and* SISSY *stay behind.*]

MR. GRADGRIND:
It was your wretched brother, Louisa?

LOUISA:
I'm afraid so, Father.

MR. GRADGRIND:
And what are we to do now? How is he to be saved from justice? In the few hours that I can possibly allow to elapse before I publish the truth and clear that poor man's name, how is he to be found? Ten thousand pounds could not effect it.

LOUISA:
Sissy has effected it, Father.

MR. GRADGRIND:
It is always you, my child!

SISSY:
We had our fears before yesterday, and when I saw you brought to the side of the litter I went to him when no one saw and told him to hide at my father's old circus. This time of year they will be near Liverpool.

MR. GRADGRIND:
Thank heaven! He may be got abroad yet.

## THE NOODLE

[*Music. Scene shifts to* BOUNDERBY's. MRS. SPARSIT *looks woefully at* BOUNDERBY.]

BOUNDERBY:
What's the matter now, ma'am?

MRS. SPARSIT:
Pray, sir, do not bite my nose off.

BOUNDERBY:
Bite your nose off, ma'am! *Your* nose!

MRS. SPARSIT:
May I ask, sir, have you been ruffled this morning?

BOUNDERBY:
Now, I'll tell you what, ma'am, I am not come here to be bullied. A female may be highly connected, but she can't be permitted to bother and badger a man in my position, and I am not going to put up with it.

MRS. SPARSIT:

Sir. It is apparent to me that I am in your way at present. I will retire to my own apartment.

BOUNDERBY:

Allow me to open the door, ma'am—

MRS. SPARSIT:

Thank you, sir; I can do it for myself—

BOUNDERBY:

You had better allow me, ma'am, because I can take the opportunity of saying a word to you before you go. Ma'am, I think you are cramped here, do you know? It appears to me that, under my humble roof, there's hardly opening enough for a lady of your genius in other people's affairs.

MRS. SPARSIT:

Really, sir?

BOUNDERBY:

I have been thinking it over, you see, since the late affairs have happened, ma'am, and it appears to my poor judgment—

MRS. SPARSIT:

Oh! Please, sir, don't disparage your judgment. Everybody knows how unerring Mr. Bounderby's judgment is. Everybody has had proofs of it. It must be the theme of general conversation.

BOUNDERBY:

It appears to me, ma'am, that a different sort of establishment altogether would bring out a lady of your powers. Such an establishment as your relation, Lady Scadger's, now. Don't you think you might find some affairs there, ma'am, to interfere with?

MRS. SPARSIT:
It never occurred to me before, sir, but now you mention it, I should think it highly probable.

BOUNDERBY:
Then suppose you try, ma'am. I really ought to apologize to you for having stood in your light so long!

MRS. SPARSIT:
Pray don't name it, sir. And as for names, a long period has elapsed since I first secretly addressed you as a Noodle. Nothing that a Noodle does can awaken surprise or indignation; the proceedings of a Noodle can only inspire contempt.

[MRS. SPARSIT *leaves*.]


## WHELP HUNTING

[*Music.* LOUISA, SISSY, *and* MR. GRADGRIND *arrive backstage at the circus and meet up with* SLEARY.]

SLEARY:
Thethilia, it doth me good to thee you.

[*They embrace.*]

Thquire, your thervant. And thith mutht be your daughter. . . .

MR. GRADGRIND:

Is my son safe?

SLEARY:

Thafe and thound! [*Pointing to the circus's onstage area*] He'th the clown with the thcarlet polka dotth. I'll bring him thtraight to you, Thquire!

[SLEARY *goes "onstage" and carries* TOM *to the circus's backstage area and to his family. The circus continues quietly in slow motion as the following scene backstage at the circus takes place.*]

MR. GRADGRIND:

How was this done?

TOM:

How was what done?

MR. GRADGRIND:

This robbery.

TOM:

I forced the safe myself overnight and shut it up ajar before I went away. I had had the key that was found made long before. I dropped it that morning that it might be supposed to have been used.

MR. GRADGRIND:

If a thunderbolt had fallen on me, it would have shocked me less than this!

TOM:

I don't see why. So many people are employed in situations of trust; so many people, out of many, will be dishonest. I have heard you talk of its being a law of nature. How can I help laws? You have comforted others with such things, Father. Comfort yourself!

MR. GRADGRIND:
You must be got to Liverpool and sent abroad.

TOM:
I suppose I must. I can't be more miserable anywhere than I have been here, ever since I can remember. That's one thing.

[SLEARY *returns to the circus's backstage area as a new act begins performing in slow motion behind the following scene.*]

MR. GRADGRIND:
Mr. Sleary, how do we get him away?

SLEARY:
There'th a coach in about ten minuteth that goeth thtraight to Liverpool. Thay farewell to your family, and tharp'th the word!

MR. GRADGRIND:
Here is your letter. All necessary means will be provided for you. Atone, by repentance and better conduct, for the shocking action you have committed and the dreadful consequences to which it has led. Give me your hand, my poor boy, and may God forgive you as I do!

[LOUISA *opens her arms to him.*]

TOM:
Not you. I don't want to have anything to say to you!

LOUISA:

Oh, Tom, Tom, do we end so, after all my love!

TOM:

Pretty love! Leaving old Bounderby to himself and packing my best friend, Mr. Harthouse, off, and going home, just when I was in the greatest danger. Pretty love that! Coming out with every word about our having gone to that place when you saw the net was gathering round me. Pretty love that! You never cared for me.

LOUISA:

Tom, I forgive you, dearest! I love you still. One day you'll be sorry to have left me so and glad to think of these my last words to you—I love you forever.

[*They all stop cold as* BITZER *enters.*]

BITZER:

I'm sorry to interfere with your plans, but I can't allow myself to be done by circus folk. I must have young Mr. Tom.

LOUISA:

No!

MR. GRADGRIND:

Bitzer, have you a heart?

BITZER:

The circulation, sir, couldn't be carried on without one.

MR. GRADGRIND:

Is it accessible to any compassionate influence?

BITZER:

It is accessible to reason, sir, and to nothing else.

[SLEARY *whispers to* SISSY, *who quietly leaves.*]

MR. GRADGRIND:

What motive can you have for preventing the escape of this wretched youth and crushing his miserable father? See his sister here; pity us!

LOUISA:

Please, Bitzer!

BITZER:

Sir, I am going to take Mr. Tom to Mr. Bounderby, where I expect to be promoted to young Mr. Tom's situation.

MR. GRADGRIND:

If this is solely a question of self-interest with you—

BITZER:

The whole social system is a question of self-interest. You taught me that at your school! Come, Mr. Tom.

[SLEARY *grabs* TOM *and drags him "onstage." Action with the magic trunk.* TOM *is put in;* SISSY *pops out;* BITZER *looks into the trunk, but* TOM *is gone.* BITZER *is shoved into the trunk and whisked offstage. The "onstage" circus ends to sounds of applause.* SLEARY, SISSY, *and the other* CIRCUS FOLK *bow.*]

SLEARY [*to the "audience"*]:
May all your dayth be thircuth dayth! Adieu, adieu, adieu!

[SLEARY *and* SISSY *rejoin* MR. GRADGRIND *and* LOUISA *"backstage"* *as the other performers run off.*]

All right, Thquire! Your thon thould be aboard a thip in no time.

MR. GRADGRIND:
Oh thank you, sir, thank you, but how did he escape?

SLEARY:
It wath magic, Thquire. . . .

MR. GRADGRIND:
Yes, of course it was! And, Mr. Sleary, I will repay you for your help.

SLEARY:
If you'll only give a thircuth a good word whenever you can, you'll more than balanthe the account. Now, Thquire, if your daughter will ethcuthe me, I thould like one parting word with you.

[SISSY *and* LOUISA *wander into the now-empty circus ring.*]

SLEARY:
Thquire, you don't need to be told that dogth ith wonderful ani-malth.

MR. GRADGRIND:
Their instinct is surprising.

SLEARY:
Whatever you call it—and I'm bletht if I know what to call it; it ith athtonithing. The way in whith a dog'll find you—the dithtanthe he'll come!

MR. GRADGRIND:

His scent being so fine.

SLEARY:

I'm bletht if I know what to call it, but I have had dogth find me, Thquire, in a way that made me think whether that dog hadn't gone to another dog and thed, "You don't happen to know a perthon of the name of Thleary, do you? A thircuth man with a lithp?" And whether that dog mightn't have thed, "I can get you hith addreth directly." Anyway, fourteen month ago, Thquire, we wath at Chethter, and one morning, there cometh into our ring, by the thtage door, a dog. He had traveled a long way; he wath in very bad condithon; he wath lame and pretty well blind. He went round to our children, one after another, ath if he wath a-theeking for a child he know'd; and then he come to me, and throwed hithelf up and thtood on hith two forelegth, wagged hith tail, and died. Thquire, that dog wath Merrylegth.

MR. GRADGRIND:

Sissy's father's dog!

SLEARY:

Now, Thquire, I can take my oath from my knowledge of that dog, that that man wath dead and buried afore that dog come back to me. Tho whether her father bathely detherted her or whether he broke hith own heart alone rather than pull her down along with him never will be known now, Thquire, till—no, not till we know how the dogth find uth out!

MR. GRADGRIND:

She keeps the bottle that he sent her for, to this hour; and she will believe in his affection to the last moment of her life.

SLEARY:

It theemth to prethent two thingth to a perthon, don't it, Thquire? One, that there ith a love in the world, not all thelf-interetht after all, but thomething very different; t'other, that love hath a way of ith own of calculating or not calculating, which ith at leatht ath hard to give a name to ath the wayth of the dogth ith!

[*The* CIRCUS FOLK *enter the ring, greet* SISSY, *and start cleaning up and moving items after their show.*]

Hey everyone, thay hello to Thithy'th Thquire!

[*The company greets* MR. GRADGRIND *and continues cleaning up and breaking down the set.*]

MR. GRADGRIND:

Thank you so much for your help!

SLEARY:

Thquire, to thee your daughter treating Thithy like a thithter, and a thithter that thee truthtth and honorth with all her heart and more ith a very pretty thight to me. Thquire, thake handth, firth and latht! Don't be croth with uth poor vagabondth. People mutht be amuthed. They can't be alwayth a-learning, nor yet they can't be alwayth a-working; they a'n't made for it. You mutht have uth, Thquire. Do the withe thing and the kind thing, too, and make the betht of uth; not the wurtht!

[*Final image: The* CIRCUS FOLK *have helped* LOUISA *climb up the web (a rope). With* SISSY *giving her instructions, she slowly starts to spin, her dark Victorian dress billowing out around her. Music. The spin gets faster; she is flying through the air as the lights fade.*]

1. Tom (Joe Sikora), Louisa (Louise Lamson), Sissy (Lauren Hirte), and Bitzer (Tony Hernandez), Lookingglass Theatre

2. Kidderminster (Philip Smith), Sleary (David Catlin), and Sissy (Lauren Hirte), Lookingglass Theatre

3. Bounderby (Troy West) and Mrs. Sparsit (Barbara Robertson), Lookingglass Theatre

4. Rachael (Eva Barr) and Stephen (David Catlin), Lookingglass Theatre

5. Sissy's Mother (Eva Barr) and Sissy's Father (Raymond Fox),
Lookingglass Theatre

6. Sissy (Lauren Hirte) and Sissy's Father (Raymond Fox), Lookingglass Theatre

7. Louisa (Louise Lamson) and Sissy (Lauren Hirte),
Lookingglass Theatre

8. Louisa (Louise Lamson), Tom (Joe Sikora), Bounderby (Troy West), Bitzer (Tony Hernandez), and Harthouse (Philip Smith), Lookingglass Theatre

9. Mrs. Sparsit (Barbara Robertson), Lookingglass Theatre

10. Louisa (Louise Lamson) and Mr. Gradgrind (Raymond Fox),
Lookingglass Theatre

1. Stephen (David Catlin), Rachael (Eva Barr), Bitzer (Tony Hernandez), Sissy (Lauren Hirte),
Louisa (Louise Lamson), and Mr. Gradgrind (Raymond Fox), Lookingglass Theatre

12. Mr. Gradgrind (Raymond Fox), Sissy (Lauren Hirte), Louisa (Louise Lamson), Tom (Joe Sikora), and circus performers (David Catlin, Eva Barr, and Barbara Robertson), Lookingglass Theatre

## ACKNOWLEDGMENTS

For their significant contributions to the development of the script, the author would like to thank the Lookingglass Theatre Artistic Development Program, especially Laura Eason, David Catlin, Phil Smith, and John Musial; assistant director Tracy Walsh; and the casts of both Chicago productions of *Hard Times*.

## ABOUT THE PLAYWRIGHT

Heidi Stillman is a writer, a director, an actor, and an ensemble member of the Lookingglass Theatre Company of Chicago, where she served as artistic director from 1997 to 2000. Her adaptation credits include the Jeff-nominated *Baron in the Trees* (with Larry DiStasi) and *The Master and Margarita*. She has appeared in more than fifteen Lookingglass world premieres and was in the original New York cast of the Tony Award–winner *Metamorphoses*.